2ND EDITION How to write & prepare

TRAINING MATERIALS

NANCY STIMSON

**KOGAN
PAGE**

How to write & prepare
TRAINING MATERIALS

To Michael, Holly and Vicky

First published in 1991
Second edition 2002
Reprinted 2005

120 Pentonville Road
London N1 9JN
UK
www.kogan-page.co.uk

22883 Quicksilver Drive
Sterling VA 20166–2012
USA

British Library Cataloguing in Publication Data

A CIP record for this book is available from the British Library.

ISBN 0 7494 3723 5

Typeset by JS Typesetting Ltd, Porthcaw, Mid Glamorgan
Printed and bound in Great Britain by Cambridge University Press

Contents

Preface

This edition has been revised throughout to take account of the transformation in what we write and read in these days of e-mails, electronic presentations and Web sites.

Technology has substantially changed the preparation, appearance and delivery of many training materials. Computer packages, 'wizards' and templates abound to assist you in developing presentations, forms, charts, letters, reports, Web pages – in fact, just about everything you may wish to write. But despite the technological wizardry, the basic principles of writing training materials do not change.

As with the previous edition, this book is aimed at providing the general trainer with an overview of how to write well the large variety of materials that trainers need to write. I hope you will find this revised edition a useful guide to writing and preparing training materials in the electronic age.

Introduction

How to write everything trainers write

As a trainer you probably think of yourself as someone who speaks to people – large seminar audiences, small workshop groups, individual managers and employees. But trainers are not just speakers; they are prolific writers too. In achieving the trainer's objective, helping someone to learn something, there are several typical stages:

- Identifying what should be done (and recording this in job descriptions, job aids, procedures manuals etc).
- Identifying what is being done, and the resulting gap often recorded in performance appraisal or other reports.
- Proposing how to resolve the gap (probably in a memo, report or other written form).
- Delivering training inputs (to the accompaniment of course notes, visuals, handouts, exercises, self-learning texts etc).
- Following-up after the training (probably with more memos or reports).

All the pieces of writing listed above are training materials. Helping both the novice and experienced trainer to write and prepare them is what this book is all about.

Trainers have special needs as writers. As we have seen, their output is considerable; they write many different kinds of documents; these go to many different readers. And, to make matters worse, trainers are also expected to be 'expert' in this as in many other fields – they may even have to run Writing Skills courses. This is expecting a lot from professionals whose own basic training usually concentrates on speaking skills.

National competency standards for trainers do acknowledge the importance of writing, stressing that written materials should be 'accurate and in a style and format appropriate to the needs and capabilities of the audience'. But even in this quotation from the UK National Standards for Training and Development, the word 'audience' reveals the bias towards face-to-face communication.

This book is an attempt to adjust the balance. It is a three-part writing resource for trainers.

Part 1 provides a brief refresher on writing principles. It examines how you can make life easy for your reader (and therefore improve your chances of achieving your objectives) by planning your writing, choosing your words, presenting the material attractively, and editing it to make sure it says and does what you want. There are a number of exercises to help you hone your skills, as well as checklists to act as memory-joggers.

Part 2 considers all the various materials trainers may write:

- job descriptions, performance standards and performance objectives, competency descriptions;
- procedures; job aids and manuals;
- forms and questionnaires;
- course notes;
- course visuals;
- course handouts;
- course exercises;
- self-learning texts;
- Web sites;
- reports, letters, memos, e-mails and minutes of meetings.

The chapters in Part 2 give practical tips on how to handle these writing tasks, using standard formats and examples.

Part 3 is for reference and for interest. It is a collection of chapters on various associated topics: source materials, legalities (copyright and data protection law), grammar, punctuation and spelling, tables and charts, and using technology. Dip into these chapters as you need them.

Part 1, together with the add-ons in Part 3, form a foundation of writing skills and knowledge which can then be applied to all the different documents that trainers write.

Writing can be a chore or it can be a delight. Enjoy your writing, and this book!

Part 1
Writing Basics

1

Writing to be Read

Summary

Writers need to be read, and therefore to make their writing attractive to readers by focusing from the reader's point of view. This is a chapter of questions, Kipling's 'six honest serving men'. Before writing, ask yourself:

- Why are you writing? What objective do you want your reader to achieve?
- Who is your reader? What do you know about him/her/them? Do multiple readers have conflicting needs?
- How do you want to write? What format and tone should you use?
- When do you write best? How can you meet your deadline?
- Where do you write best?
- What should you include? How should you structure your material?

Writers need to be read

Do you read everything that piles up in your in-tray? Do all your intended readers actually read everything you have written? The amount of paper going straight from in-tray to wastepaper bin represents a horrific cost, in financial and environmental terms, and in wasted writer-hours.

Writers need to be read. And, just as important, they need to be understood correctly. For the reality of your communication, of course, lies not in what you wanted to write, or even what you did write, but in what your reader understood.

Let us see what, from a reader's point of view, are the barriers to reading and understanding:

- The reader has too much else to do.
- The document seems irrelevant to his or her needs.
- The length (or even weight!) of the document is off-putting. We all tend to deal with short matters first, and push the long reports to the bottom of the pile.
- The document is visually unattractive, with long paragraphs, small margins and no headings.
- The content is poorly structured, with no logical links between points.
- The document contains too many long words and long sentences, including jargon and technical terms.

As a writer you can and must break down these barriers. You can even influence your intended reader's workload by considering, before you pick up your pen: 'Should I write at all? Why?' There are good reasons for writing:

- to establish a permanent record;
- to make the message more formal;
- to convey the same message to many people;
- to provide low-cost training – writing training material can be fairly cheap, at least in direct costs;
- to achieve reasonably fast delivery and response (using fax or e-mail) or more delayed delivery and response (via postal systems), whichever you want.

However, in many cases, a telephone call or quick face-to-face chat is more effective. If so, don't write; talk.

Readers and objectives

Once you have decided that you *should* be writing, your next question is not 'To whom should I write?' but 'Who needs to read this?' The difference is more than just one of phraseology – it is one of approach, of putting your reader first and seeing through his or her eyes rather than your own, probably the single golden rule which will make any communication most effective.

Effectiveness, achieving your objective, is the sole reason for communicating at all. You do need to have that objective clearly in your mind. Think back to your last piece of writing. What was your objective? When asked this question, even experienced trainers, accustomed to expressing training objectives in terms of trainees' desired behaviour, are liable to answer 'I wanted to say. . .' But behavioural objectives are just as important for writing as for training courses – being clear in your own mind specifically what you want the reader to do is the first step to having that happen.

As with training objectives, the key to formulating behavioural objectives for your writing lies in making your reader the subject of the sentence, and then using an 'action verb'. So start your objectives with the formula: 'After reading this, my reader will…' and continue with an action verb, not the vague 'know', 'understand', 'appreciate' which so easily spring to mind, but the specific 'decide', 'carry out', 'complete', 'remember'.

For example, the objectives of a joining letter to managers nominated to attend a presentation skills course could be as follows.

'Readers (ie the managers nominated to attend the writing skills course) will:

- attend the course;
- want to attend the course;
- know when and where to go, and what to bring with them;
- identify their personal needs for the course;
- prepare themselves for the course;
- know what to expect from the course;
- be prepared to admit and address their fears and weaknesses;
- let the organizers know if they cannot attend the course.'

The behavioural nature of the objective may be obvious ('attend the course') or less so ('*want* to attend the course', and show this in behaviour, however subtly). As a bottom-line objective, you should always want all your readers to remember what you have written or, at least, *that* you have written something on the subject. If even that is not really necessary for some readers (or more likely non-readers), remove them from your distribution list. Their in-trays will be grateful. Having a single reader simplifies your job as a writer; it is, however, comparatively rare. Even a letter or memo addressed to one person may, predictably, be shown to others. Whether you have one reader or several, the more you know about them, the better. First of all, their names. 'Dear Sir or Madam' letters should be avoided wherever possible.

Then consider:

- How well do they understand your language (both the English language and your technical jargon)?
- How much do they know about the subject?
- What are their concerns and prejudices likely to be?
- What authority do they have?
- What could prevent them from achieving your objectives?

If you cannot answer these questions, a little initial research will save a lot of later frustration.

Sometimes, if you have multiple readers, their needs may conflict. You may be able to accommodate this in your writing, for instance, by putting background details, needed by only *some* readers of a report, in an appendix. You may concentrate on meeting the needs of your most important reader, important not necessarily in status terms, but as the person who will achieve your objective. You may write different documents – the full report for the person who needs to know all the details, and a summary, or a note explaining what the report covers and where it is filed, for the person who only needs to know that it has been written. Or you may just have to live with the conflict (for example, where one trainee may need the course-joining letter to stimulate his or her excitement and another to reassure his or her fears) and mitigate the effects by talking to the people concerned.

Planning

All the above concerns are part of your initial planning. They answer Kipling's **'Why?'** and **'Who?'** questions. He had four others:

How? What format you should choose, eg letter, memo, report, is also important. Part 2 of this book gives tips on how to handle the different writing tasks you may need to perform. 'How' should also cover the tone you want to convey – formal or friendly, rational or inspirational, decisive or questioning.

When? If you have a deadline, meet it. If you do not have a deadline, set yourself one and meet it. To see if the deadline is realistic, work backwards from it, and judge how long you should allow for revision, typing, drafting, planning and research. Do you have enough time? If not, can you change your deadline? If not, what can you reduce? Maybe someone else can do part of your research, maybe you will have to limit the scope of what you cover. But, for your reader's sake (and therefore your own), meet your deadline.

Also consider which time of day you work best. Some of us are larks, wide awake and fully functioning in the early morning; others are owls, stimulated in the evening. Whichever you are, choose if you can that time for writing.

Where? Balance the peacefulness of writing at home, without the distractions of work-based telephone calls and interruptions, with the convenience of having all your information available at the workplace. An empty training room, or even someone else's office could prove the ideal solution. And, wherever you write, set up your environment to make it as easy as possible – comfortable chair, good lighting, telephone off-the-hook, reference materials to hand.

What? What material, what points do you include? And in what order?

Structure

Firstly, decide what your main point is and at what stage you want to make it. It often seems logical to leave it until the end, and build up to it with supporting data. But your reader may not read to the end. Try to make your main point as early as you can, maybe even in the first paragraph of a memo or letter, or at the beginning of the summary of a report.

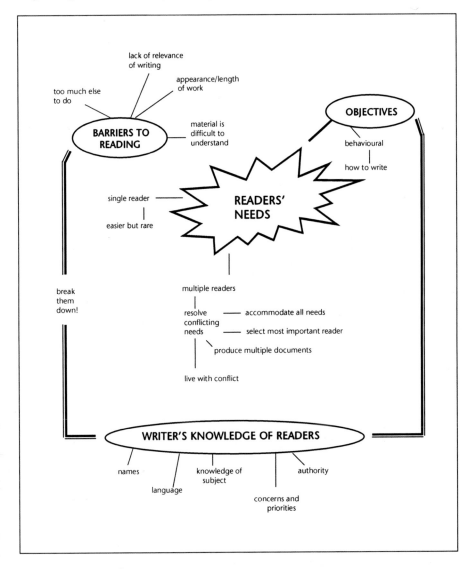

Figure 1.1 Mind map

Then consider the rest of your content from the reader's position. For each item, ask yourself: 'Does my reader need to know this? Why?' The order of your material, too, should depend on the reader and your objective.

There are various techniques to help you structure your writing. The simplest is merely to list your points and juggle them around, either by numbering your list or, physically, by writing each point on adhesive stickers. These points then form separate sections or paragraphs. Other structuring techniques use visual effects (placing, colour, size, pictures) to help you recognize links between points. Decision trees, flowcharts and 'mind maps' are examples of these.

Checklist: Writing to be read

Before starting to write, how well do you consider:	OK	Could be better	Should be better
● whether you should write at all?	—	—	—
● who your reader is?	—	—	—
● whether you know enough about your reader?	—	—	—
● what your objective is, in behavioural terms?	—	—	—
● what your reader's needs are?	—	—	—
● how to resolve the conflicting needs of multiple readers?	—	—	—
● what format you want to use?	—	—	—
● what tone you want to use?	—	—	—
● how to meet your deadline?	—	—	—
● when you write best?	—	—	—
● where you write best?	—	—	—
● what your main point is, and where you will place it?	—	—	—
● what other points you will include?	—	—	—
● how you will structure them?	—	—	—

2

Choosing your Words

Summary

Despite all your planning, sometimes the words just will not come. Tactics for overcoming writer's block include: postponement; subdividing the writing task; starting in the middle or at the end; systematically expanding 'brainstormed' ideas; dictating; typing (if you are used to writing by hand) or writing (if you are used to a keyboard).

This chapter looks at the importance of writing style. Tools to help you find the right word include dictionaries and thesauruses. Misuse of words leads to confusion. The best writing is composed of short, simple, familiar words in short, simple sentences (keep it short and simple – KISS). Some useful guidelines are:

- Eliminate redundancies.
- Avoid jargon.
- Use the positive rather than the negative.
- Use concrete rather than abstract nouns.
- Use verbs rather than nouns.
- Use active rather than passive verb forms.
- Use the first and second person pronouns ('I' and 'you').
- Use non-sexist language.

The complexity of a piece of writing may be measured by Robert Gunning's FOG Index, which is based on word and sentence length.

Writer's block

Blank mind and blank paper – a state familiar to all writers. However well you have planned your writing, sometimes those critical first words just will not come.

Probably the best way of handling this situation is, if possible, to postpone writing – sleep on it, take a walk round the block, or even take a bath. It was not through chance that Archimedes cried 'Eureka' in his bath: immersion in water produces physical and mental relaxation, which allows the super-efficient unconscious mind to resolve any outstanding problems.

Other tactics, more acceptable in the workplace, include subdividing the writing task, and starting in the middle or at the end – anywhere apart from the blocked beginning. Another approach is to 'brainstorm'. Give yourself a time limit (say 5–10 minutes) and write down as many phrases, thoughts, images as you can think of. Do not try to revise or polish these: you are aiming for quantity, not quality. Having got some material, you can then build systematically on this and on the plan you have already produced, expanding points, linking up your 'brainstormed' words and ideas, and adding examples.

If all else fails, throw away the pen and paper. Some people find it less off-putting to type directly onto a typewriter or word processor screen. (Contrari-wise, if you normally spend your life glued to the keyboard, try the low-tech approach.) Some people also prefer to talk, dictating to a tape recorder or simply explaining the material to a friend.

Finding the 'right' word

Once you have started, do not stop to hunt down an elusive term. First drafts are not meant to be perfect. If you are stuck on a word, leave a gap or put down an approximation, and go on. When you come to revise your draft later, you may find the exact word leaps out at you. If not, tools such as dictionaries, synonym dictionaries (as used by crossword puzzle addicts), or a thesaurus can be a great help.

These books are also useful for expanding your vocabulary. It is estimated that the vocabulary of English-speaking adults may vary from 12,000 to 30,000 words. Browsing in dictionaries can also bring surprising revelations about words you thought you understood.

Misunderstood and misused words can be highly dangerous. If I *realize* that I do not understand the word 'continually' which you have included in safety instructions, I can ask you to explain it. But if I believe it means 'constantly' or 'without stopping', and you (correctly) intend it to mean 'repeatedly', we have a problem. 'Evacuate the building when the fire alarm sounds continually' is a recipe for chaos and disaster.

Many words are commonly misused, sometimes even changing the meaning of the sentence completely. Here are some pairs of words which are often confused. What do they mean?

1	affect / effect	2	alternate / alternative
3	bi- /semi-	4	complement / compliment
5	ie / eg	6	disinterested / uninterested
7	imply / infer	8	principal / principle
9	practise / practice	10	lie / lay

1 **Affect** is a verb meaning 'have an effect on'. **Effect** is both a noun meaning 'result' and a verb meaning 'cause' or 'bring about'.

'The budget limitations affected all departments. The main effect was a ten per cent salary cut for all staff, which effected a dramatic increase in staff turnover.'

2 **Alternate** is both a verb meaning to 'take it in turn' and an adjective meaning 'every other'. **Alternative** is normally a noun meaning 'choice'. It is also used as an adjective meaning 'other', sometimes creating an unnecessary repetition. (There is no difference between 'The alternative is. . .' and 'The alternative option is. . .'.)

'Until an alternative solution is found, Ann and John will carry out the receptionist's duties on alternate days.'
'Until another alternative is found, Ann and John will alternate as receptionist.'

3 **Bi**- means 'every two' (days, weeks, months etc). **Semi**- means 'half'.

'Semi-menstrual meetings are held bi-weekly.'
(However, 'biannual' means 'twice a year' or 'half-yearly'; 'biennial means 'every two years'.)

4 **Complement** is a noun or verb that refers to 'making something complete'. **Compliment** is a noun or verb meaning 'praise'.

'Frequent compliments to employees for good work will complement a supervisor's other efforts to improve performance.'

5 **ie** is an abbreviation meaning 'that is'. **eg** is an abbreviation meaning 'for example'.

'The role of the trainer, ie someone who trains others as a part of his or her job, may be performed by many different people, eg managers, supervisors, colleagues.'

6 **Disinterested** means 'without ulterior motive'. **Uninterested** means 'bored' or 'unreceptive'.

'Although it was a disinterested piece of advice, the employee remained uninterested.'

7 **Imply** means 'suggest'. **Infer** means 'deduce'.

'The consultant implied that we should first tackle our technical training deficiencies; however, we inferred from our internal surveys that poor communication was a greater problem.'

8 **Principal** is an adjective meaning 'chief' or 'most important'. It is also a noun meaning the 'principal person'. **Principle** is a noun meaning 'fundamental rule'.

'The school principal's principal task that day was to work out budgetary control principles.'

9 **Practise** is a verb and **practice** is a noun (except in US English where **practice** is both verb and noun – see Chapter 17).

'The girl did her piano practice although she did not enjoy practising.'

10 **Lie** is an intransitive verb meaning 'assume a lying position'. **Lay**, as a verb, has various meanings, but the confusion with **lie** arises because **lay** is a transitive verb meaning 'to place in a lying position'. It is also the past tense of **lie.**

'"I will lay the papers straight so that they lie tidily on the desk," he said. He then lay down for a rest.'

Figure 2.1 What do they mean?

KISS

We have already established that the best way to avoid misunderstandings is to choose your words carefully and to keep it simple and short (KISS).

Polysyllables are cumbersome – aren't they? People sometimes think, however, that long words and sentences look more impressive and professional than short ones. Let Winston Churchill, the ultimate impressive, professional communicator, rebut that (Figure 2.2).

The Plain English Campaign originated to rid official language of its 'gobbledegook', and public documents certainly have improved. For instance, (although readers struggling to complete income tax self-assessment questionnaires may doubt this) the latest instructions for completing income tax forms are models of simplicity and clarity compared to those of earlier years.

National newspapers have followed suit and run competitions to expose particularly tortuous examples of commercialese. Some of the competitions invite

To do our work, we all have to read a mass of papers. Nearly all of them are far too long. This wastes time, while energy has to be spent in looking for the essential points. I ask my colleagues and their staffs to see to it that their reports are shorter.

(i)   The aim should be reports which set out the main points in a series of short crisp paragraphs.

(ii) If a report relies on a detailed analysis of some complicated factors, or on statistics, these should be set out in an appendix.

(iii) Often the occasion is best met by submitting not a full-dress report, but an aide-memoire consisting of headings only, which can be expanded orally if needed.

(iv) Let us have an end of such phrases as these:
'It is also of importance to bear in mind the following considerations. . .' or
'Consideration should be given to the possibility of carrying into effect. . .'
Most of these woolly phrases are mere padding, which can be left out altogether, or replaced by a single word. Let us not shrink from using the short, expressive phrase, even if it is conversational.

Reports drawn up on the lines I propose may at first seem rough as compared with the flat surface of officialese jargon, but the saving in time will be great, while the discipline of setting out the real points concisely will prove an aid to clearer thinking.

10 Downing Street
9th August 1940   WSC

Figure 2.2 It was ever thus. . .

readers to rewrite these passages in comprehensible English. It is surprising how easy it can be to eliminate redundancies and avoid long, convoluted words and sentences.

Short, simple words are easy both to write and understand.

Useful guidelines

Jargon

Everyone knows that jargon is bad – but it is not, necessarily. Using your readers' jargon is an excellent way of making them feel you understand their needs, and goes a long way to persuading them to accept your suggestions.

Jargon is merely technical terminology. It enables you to communicate technical information shortly and precisely, *provided your reader understands it.*

Don't write this:	But this:
Along the lines of. . .	Like
In the majority of instances. . .	Usually
Give consideration to. . .	Consider
A large number of. . .	Many
In spite of the fact that. . .	Although
During the period that. . .	While
Rectangular in shape. . .	Rectangular
The month of December. . .	December
In order to. . .	To
Recur again. . .	Recur
Entirely completed. . .	Completed
In the not too distant future. . .	Soon
On the part of. . .	By
It would seem reasonable to believe. . .	I believe
The data appears to indicate. . .	I think

Figure 2.3 KISS words

Jargon which is not generally understood, however, should be avoided; it leaves your reader confused, irritated and often suspicious of your motives. Even worse is jargon which can be misunderstood, for instance words used in a technical sense which have a slightly different everyday meaning.

Much of the trainer's jargon falls into this category, eg 'facilitate', 'reinforcement', 'feedback', 'model', 'counselling', even 'needs' and 'learning'. Beware statements like: 'Reinforcement of the learning is facilitated by the use of feedback, models, and needs-based counselling'!

Positives and negatives

As trainers, we are all very much accustomed to phrasing negative comments positively, sometimes too much so. As one never-to-be-forgotten student once said to me, 'Please don't keep saying "That's interesting" when you mean "That's wrong"!' Nevertheless, positive talking and writing does work. You are much likelier to discover 'creative' solutions, if you refer to 'challenges' and 'opportunities' than if you talk about 'problems'. Positive forms of speech are also much easier to understand and more persuasive than negative ones.

Contrast: 'Please call me if. . .' and 'Please do not hesitate to call me if. . .'.

Contrast: 'I will return your call at once' and 'I will not delay in returning your call'.

Double and triple negatives can totally obscure your meaning. Take this example: 'There is no reason to doubt that his request will not be granted' – well, will it be granted or not?

Concrete and abstract nouns

Another concept familiar to trainers is the power of the concrete, visual image. I am certainly well aware of it – why, then, have I just, automatically, written 'concept', 'power' and 'image', instead of: 'Trainers also know how well people remember pictures'?

The principal reason is that we tend to *think* in abstractions, and then naturally write down our thoughts in the same words. The trouble is that abstractions, being 'thinking' words, are more likely to have subtly different meanings for different people. For instance, you may have thought I meant: 'Trainers also know how easily pictures influence people'. In fact, I may not even be quite sure of my own meaning. Abstractions are such convenient 'labels' for thoughts, that we often attach them too quickly, and this actually stops us from fully under-standing and developing our own thoughts.

Expressing abstract ideas in concrete words is a knack which improves with practice. Here are a few examples of overworked abstractions together with more precise and concrete substitutes:

facilities	not 'refreshment facilities' but 'coffee machine'.
communication	not 'written communication' but 'report'.
procedures	not 'financial recording procedures' but 'bookkeeping'.
condition	not 'error condition' but 'mistake'.
arrangements	not 'lunch arrangements' but 'sandwiches'.
situation	not 'unfavourable meteorological situation' but 'rain'.

Look back on a few of your recent reports and create your own blacklist of the abstractions you favour.

Verbs and nouns

Another way of reducing abstractions and making your writing more vivid is to carry the sense of your phrase in the verb rather than in nouns.

help	not 'be of assistance'.
tell	not 'give information'.
change	not 'carry out alterations'.

Active and passive verbs

This is probably the easiest and most effective 'quick fix' of all for making your writing strong and persuasive. There is a tradition for managers, including training managers, to write reports using the passive voice. Take, for example, the following:

'An investigation of needs was performed and it was then decided that a two-day training course would be prepared and run, within which the issue of improving managers' negotiation skills would be addressed.'

You could equally well write:

'I investigated the negotiation skill needs of managers, and will prepare and run a two-day training course to meet those needs.'

The second passage in fact gives more information than the first, specifying who has done or will do what. That may be one of the reasons for the popularity of the passive − writers can hide behind the welter of words, without actually committing themselves personally to doing anything. Of course, that is precisely the impression that comes across to the reader. . .

'I' and 'you'

Using the active voice forces use of the pronouns 'I', 'you', 'we', 'they' etc. (Watch 'we' and 'they' which again are good camouflage words.) It may be appropriate in a progress report to use 'I' repeatedly. In a letter or memo intended to persuade, sell or influence, however, the most valuable pronoun is 'you'.

'You explained your managers' problems with negotiating. I will prepare and run a two-day training course to meet your needs' is subtly different from the earlier version above.

'He' and 'she'

'You' also gets round some of the problems of non-sexist language. 'He or she', 's/he', 'he/she' all read awkwardly and are best avoided if possible. You can sometimes use the plural 'they'; you can sometimes recast the sentence completely; but watch the dangers of abstractions and passive verbs. Here are some variations:

'A trainer may feel that he needs to impress his participants.'
'A trainer may feel that [he or she] / [s/he] / [he/she] needs to impress [his or her] / [his/her] participants.'
'Trainers may feel that they need to impress their participants.'
'You, as a trainer, may feel you need to impress your participants.'
'A trainer may consider impressing participants important.'

Make life easy for your readers. Which version do you prefer?

1   Computer equipment is available to us through a variety of hardware manu-facturer supply outlets. (14 words)
or
     We have several computer suppliers. (5 words)
2   Due consideration has been given to the question of the comparative desirability of A over B, concluding that this should be resolved on a direct cost basis. (27 words)
or
     We should choose the cheaper of A or B. (9 words)
3   Communication difficulties are being experienced in interface situations between the Marketing and Accounts functions. (14 words)
or
     Marketing and Accounts do not talk to each other. (9 words)
4   It is felt by the task force that, as a first step, a proper analysis of the disciplinary procedures should be conducted. (22 words)
or
     The task force want to analyse disciplinary procedures first. (9 words)
5   The impossibility of the proposition is evident. (7 words)
or
     It is impossible. (3 words)
6   The nature of the location is such as to produce an atmosphere of relaxation and tranquility. (16 words)
or
     It is a peaceful place. (5 words)

Figure 2.4 KISS sentences

FOG Index

Having KISSed your language, you may want to see how successful you were. A handy tip is to try reading your draft aloud. Does it 'sound wrong' – is your tongue tripping over awkward words; do you run out of breath halfway through the sentence? Then run a more systematic test.

Robert Gunning's FOG Index is a convenient way of checking how simple your writing is. It is based on word and sentence length, and includes a factor to make it represent the approximate years of schooling needed to understand the language easily. The lower the FOG Index, the simpler the passage. Most classic writing has a low FOG Index (7 or 8); much business writing scores 17+! A good target is 12.

To calculate your FOG Index:

- Take a 100-word sample and identify the average number of words per sentence (ending in a full stop or a colon or semi-colon.)
- Count also the number of polysyllables (words with three or more syllables) in the 100 words, excluding capitalized words and verb forms where the third syllable is -ing, -es, or -ed (eg carrying, attaches, committed).
- Add the average sentence length to the number of polysyllables and multiply by 0.4.

As an example, the FOG Index of Churchill's memo which I quoted earlier is calculated as follows:

Average sentence length – 18 words

Polysyllables – 21 in whole memo, ie 9 per 100 words

(18 + 9) x 0.4 = a FOG Index of 11, which means that most school-leavers should be able to understand it.

Checklist: Choosing your words

Do you:

	OK	Could be better	Should be better
● Get the words flowing by:			
– doing something else?	–	–	–
– subdividing the writing task?	–	–	–
– starting at the middle/end?	–	–	–
– 'brainstorming' ideas?	–	–	–
– dictating?	–	–	–
– typing?	–	–	–
– writing by hand?	–	–	–
● Use dictionaries to:			
– check your meaning?	–	–	–
– browse through word meanings?	–	–	–
● Remember KISS and:			
– eliminate redundancies?	–	–	–
– avoid inappropriate use of jargon?	–	–	–
– avoid clichés?	–	–	–
– use positive not negative phrases?	–	–	–
– use concrete not abstract nouns?	–	–	–
– use verbs not nouns?	–	–	–
– use active not passive verbs?	–	–	–
– use 'I' and 'you'?	–	–	–
– use non-sexist language?	–	–	–

3

Presenting your Material

Summary

Layout is your responsibility as a writer; it is also your opportunity, as presentation makes an immense difference to how readable and persuasive your writing is. Points to consider are:

- white space;
- paragraphs;
- headings;
- numbering systems and lists;
- emphasis;
- colour;
- using pictures;
- presenting numerical information.

Similar principles apply to presenting material for electronic delivery. However, they need to be adapted to the particular medium (eg e-mail, on-screen presentation or Web page). Advances in technology make it easy to achieve a much more sophisticated presentation of material than in the past, but this should never be allowed to detract from your writing objective.

How much does presentation matter?

It is a cliché of modern marketing that an article can, and even should, cost many times more to package than to produce. Appearance may not be all, but it certainly makes a great difference, and one that can profitably be measured in increased sales. In another context, politicians, too, play the 'image' game.

Research into interviewing practices has similarly shown that many interview decisions are heavily influenced by first impressions.

The same is true with written material. Professional-looking presentation goes a long way to persuading your reader of your professionalism. Layout which is easy to look at encourages your reader to look and read.

How much consideration do you give to the appearance of your material? Leaving layout to a typist or IT professional, or to a company 'house style', is to abandon your responsibility and your opportunity.

Considerations for your presentation

White space

Probably the most influential factor in capturing and keeping your reader's attention is what you don't write – the white space surrounding your words. A perennial advertising favourite, even preferred to dazzling colour and animation, *white space works.*

Ways of including white space are:

- gaps between letters (eg l e t t e r s);
- gaps between words;
- gaps between lines and paragraphs;
- length of paragraphs;
- gaps at the top and bottom of the page;
- margin widths;
- indentation;
- centring text.

These spacing possibilities can easily be controlled with word processing packages.

Paragraphs

Paragraphing, of course, does more than just increase white space. It should not be a matter of chance or whim, as good paragraphing can make your material much easier for your reader to follow. There are two straightforward guidelines:

Paragraph length. Each paragraph should cover a single main issue. An average of around six to eight lines per paragraph is about right for most business writing.

However, that average can, and should, encompass a range of one to twenty lines, depending on the issue being discussed.

Signposting. Make the first sentence of each paragraph preview, summarize or lead into that paragraph's main point. The busy reader can then get the sense of the whole passage by scanning these first sentences. This sounds contrived but, in fact, it comes easily and naturally.

The passage below is the unparagraphed version of the section in this chapter headed 'How much does presentation matter?' How would you paragraph it? Check the original to see the effects of the first-sentence signposts.

It is a cliché of modern marketing that an article can, and even should, cost many times more to package than to produce. Appearance may not be all, but it certainly makes a great difference, and one that can profitably be measured in increased sales. In an other context, politicians, too, play the 'image' game. Research into interviewing practices has similarly shown that many interview decisions are heavily influenced by first impressions. The same is true with written material. Professional-looking presentation goes a long way to persuading your reader of your professionalism. Layout which is easy to look at encourages your reader to look and read. How much consideration do you give to the appearance of your material? Leaving layout to a typist or IT professional, or a company 'house style', is to abandon your responsibility and your opportunity.

Figure 3.1 Paragraphing exercise

Headings

These, even more than first-sentence signposts, direct the reader's attention to the major issues. They are the reader's road map, showing the overall structure of the document. Good headings are brief (half to three-quarters of a line at most), specific ('Miscellaneous' is not a very helpful heading), and mutually exclusive (the same point should not fall under several headings). Single paragraphs do not normally justify separate headings, but this obviously depends on the content.

Numbering systems and lists

Whether or not headings are used, it is often helpful to number sections and subsections. Two numbering systems are common:

Numeric:	Alphanumeric:
1 Section	A Section
1.1 Subsection	1 Subsection
1.1.1 Point	(a) Point
1.1.1.1 Sub-point	(i) Sub-point

The numeric system is the more useful for cross-referencing.

With either system, four levels of subdivision should be the maximum, and even that may leave your reader struggling to disentangle your connections.

Items in lists can be numbered according to whichever system you have chosen. Alternatively, you can highlight them with bullet points. (You can use open or filled circles or squares, dashes, asterisks, hash signs, or even arrows or flower shapes, according to your fancy – not all of them, however!) You can even omit these preliminaries altogether.

Different layouts can give more or less emphasis to lists. You do not have to start at the left-hand margin; indenting and even centring the items, particularly short unbulleted ones, can be very effective.

Emphasis

To ensure that the reader who only scans your material does not miss any important points, you may want to emphasize these visually. There are many ways of doing this, including using:

CAPITAL LETTERS	*italics*
<u>underlining</u>	different font sizes
bold type	different fonts
l e t t e r s p a c i n g	asterisk ★ signposts ★
borders and boxes	shadow effects
colour	animation effects (if you are using electronic media)
You may even	★★★ *C O M B I N E S T Y L E S* ★★★

But be wary – too much variety dazzles the eye and disengages the brain. Moderation and consistency are often to be preferred.

Colour and animation

Moderation and consistency are particularly important given the infinite variety of colour and animation effects available for those using electronic word and data processing. Playing with colour schemes, animation and multimedia can be great fun, and the appropriate use of these can greatly enhance the professional presentation of your work. However, they do have disadvantages.

Searching for the 'right' border, background or colour scheme can take a lot of time, which might be better spent on ensuring that your message is truly meeting your readers' needs. Animation and multimedia effects also take up huge amounts of file space, making files difficult to send and slow to download.

Having said this, simple but bold use of colour in pictures, and in particular the use of colour rather than black-and-white photographs, makes great impact and adds clarity to the message you are trying to convey.

These days, colour reproduction onto white paper is easily available, but colour copying may still be considered too slow or expensive for bulk copies. As an alternative, copying black-and-white material onto coloured paper is a cheap and effective way of splitting up and emphasizing different sections of training manuals or even reports.

Pictures

Another acronym is PUP – please use pictures. These may be charts or tables; they may also be photographs (colour really is best here, but modern photo-copiers do reproduce photographs adequately into black-and-white) or other illustrations. Anything which can save a thousand words has to be welcome, but pictures have other advantages too:

- They attract the reader's eye and, therefore, attention.
- They are often remembered better than words.
- They convey a professional image.

See Chapters 9 and 18 for ideas about illustrations.

Numerical information

Finally, I want to consider briefly the presentation of numerical information. The only thing more daunting, for many readers, than a page crammed with closely-written text is one crammed with numbers. Only include the few numbers that are truly essential to your argument.

If possible, display these numbers in chart or tabular form (see Chapter 18 for more details on this); banish them to an appendix rather than incorporating them in the text; and remember KISS.

Use short numbers – substitute the word 'million' for a string of noughts, or indicate the order of magnitude of the figures at the beginning of a chart or table.

Use simplified numbers – quote 'ballpark' figures, averages and mid-points, and round to three or at most four significant figures (eg not £6,478,329, but £6.48 million or even £6.5 million.) The loss of accuracy is usually more than balanced by the increase in understanding.

PC presentation

Much writing these days is actually read from a computer screen. E-mail, Web pages and on-screen presentations are obvious examples, but many files and documents are accessed electronically instead of or as well as being printed. This means that your reader may be seeing a full A4 printed page, a full screen presentation, or maybe a reduced size screen image. Many effects which are successful on paper can be very confusing if you can only see part of the page on the screen. And conversely, many electronic techniques are simply not possible to represent well in paper format. It is essential to identify how your writing is *most likely* to be read, and adapt your presentation to that medium.

Here are a few tips for adapting paper-based material for on-screen viewing:

- Landscape rather than portrait orientation is better, if it is important that readers should be able to see the whole page at a time.
- Use a large enough font so that the writing is easily readable, even with reduced magnification to allow the whole page to be seen on-screen at one time.
- Save your document in such a way that, when it is reopened by your reader, it will automatically be presented in the right view and orientation and with the right level of magnification for easy reading.
- Hide tools and effects which can distract your reader (eg spelling and grammar checks, page breaks).

When adapting screen-based material for paper presentation:

- Convert to portrait orientation and check page breaks. If portrait orientation would detract from the material, ensure that the print setting is correctly set to 'landscape'.
- Review and revise any sections of the material which depend on colour or animation techniques to convey their message.
- If colour printing will be too time-consuming or impractical, recolour material into black-and-white, or set print settings to grey-scale or black-and-white.

Checklist: Presenting your material

Do you:

	OK	Could be better	Should be better
consider the appearance of your material?	–	–	–
plan the use of white space?	–	–	–
have one main topic per paragraph?	–	–	–
begin each paragraph with 'signpost' sentences?	–	–	–
use headings?	–	–	–
use a consistent numbering system?	–	–	–
display lists effectively?	–	–	–
include only essential numbers?	–	–	–
present numbers simply?	–	–	–
use charts and tables?	–	–	–
include detailed information in appendices?	–	–	–
use emphasis and appropriate colour effects?	–	–	–
use appropriate animation effects?	–	–	–
use pictures?	–	–	–
adapt your work to paper or on-screen presentation?	–	–	–

4

Editing and Revision

Summary

Review and revision are integral parts of the writing task. The most important review is the one from your reader's standpoint, assessing how well your writing will achieve its objective. If possible get other people to perform this review in order to get different reactions.

The reviewer's ABC stands for accuracy (of facts, and basic proofreading of grammar, punctuation and spelling), brevity and clarity.

First review level

You have written your final words; the report, case study or job description has been typed; you sigh with relief that your writing task is finished. But it probably is not. Only for short, straightforward documents should the first draft also be the last. The opportunity to review, edit and revise is one great advantage that writing has over speech. However, to be valuable, the review needs to be seen as an integral part of the writing operation, to be planned and tackled systematically.

There are different levels of review. The first and most important is to consider how well the document will achieve your objective. Will your reader be willing and able to:

- carry out your instructions?
- agree with your conclusions?
- support your request for a bigger budget, or whatever your aim is?

Try to dissociate yourself from your own position and put yourself in your reader's place. Ask yourself these questions:

- What does your reader need to know in order to achieve your objective? Have you included it?
- In what order will he or she want to consider the points? Have you followed that order?
- Will your reader understand your language? Have you eliminated or explained all your jargon? Have you used your reader's jargon?
- What do you expect your reader to do next? Have you said so?

It is better not to carry out this review immediately you have finished writing. Leave it for an hour or two, or even overnight if you can, and you will feel less proprietorial about your work, and more prepared to cut and change as drastically as necessary.

On the other hand, do not continually make minor alterations which are no great improvement on the original. Such alterations may be much easier with word processors, but they are still not worth your time.

Getting one or more other people to review the work for you avoids the danger of your merely repeating your previous thought patterns. It also much increases the likelihood that you will, between you, properly anticipate your reader's response, since a good reviewer will not necessarily agree with you, but will offer you a different perspective. However galling it may be to have your careful arguments rejected, it is better if they are rejected by your reviewer than by your real reader. Be grateful, and seek out that reviewer again.

ABC

A stands for accuracy

First, accuracy of facts. Check your sources. Are you making any assumptions, and if so are they valid? Are your numbers right? And any names? What about views or actions attributed to other people? These are all points which are likely to be noticed if incorrect, and to affect your reader's reaction.

Then comes the basic proofreading for errors of grammar, punctuation and spelling. Most word processors can check spelling. However, their dictionaries are limited and they only identify spellings not found in the dictionary. This means they will throw up as errors many correct words, and ignore words which exist in the dictionary but are incorrectly spelt in their context, eg 'to' instead of 'too'. If in doubt about a word or construction, look it up. And have standard reference works and dictionaries to hand before you begin, or you will be tempted not to bother.

Areas where mistakes are most commonly made are:

- beginnings;
- endings;
- near other errors;
- small words;
- additions and corrections.

These are all worth double-checking, as are:

- names;
- addresses;
- numbers;
- dates;
- section numbering;
- lines or paragraphs starting with the same word (often omitted by mistake – guard against this by reading the text aloud);
- consistency of punctuation and layout.

It often helps to proofread with a partner, especially if the material contains tables or strings of numbers. Frequent breaks improve attentiveness.

B stands for brevity

Is every point you make worth making? Keep asking yourself, 'so what?' and drop the passages which do not add to your argument. Strike out redundant phrases and clichés, making every word earn its place.

Check also for your 'pet' words. We all have them – words like 'absolutely', 'really', 'actually', 'however', 'therefore' or phrases like 'by the way', 'as a result', and so on. There is nothing wrong with these words and phrases except that we overuse them, often without realizing it. Again, this is where it is very useful to have someone else read your writing.

C stands for clarity

Check the FOG Index of your writing to test how intelligible it is; examine the layout to see how clear and readable it looks; and read the work aloud to make sure it sounds sensible.

Checklist: Editing and revision

Do you:

	OK	Could be better	Should be better
review your work?	—	—	—
get other people to review it?	—	—	—
review from the reader's standpoint?	—	—	—
revise as drastically as necessary?	—	—	—
avoid constant, minor alterations?	—	—	—
check your facts?	—	—	—
check your grammar?	—	—	—
check your punctuation?	—	—	—
check your spelling?	—	—	—
double-check error-prone parts?	—	—	—
proofread with a partner?	—	—	—
ask yourself 'so what?' for each point?	—	—	—
eliminate redundancies?	—	—	—
check your FOG Index?	—	—	—
check your layout?	—	—	—
read your writing aloud?	—	—	—

Part 2
What Trainers Write

5

Job Descriptions, Performance Standards, Performance Objectives and Competency Descriptions

Summary

- Job descriptions give a brief yet complete picture of the purpose and functions of a job. To be useful they should be kept 'live' and up to date.
- Performance standards identify how well a job should be done. They measure competent performance and focus on the results of the activity. Measures should ideally be quantitative, but that is not always possible. Express qualitative measures as clearly and unambiguously as possible.
- Performance objectives refer to one-off tasks and projects. They resemble performance standards in intent and form, except that they must have a target date for achievement of each objective.
- Competency descriptions describe the skills and behaviours required for competent performance.

Job descriptions

Job descriptions have a number of purposes:

- to ensure that the job holder and manager understand the job in the same way;

- to provide information about the job to 'outsiders', for instance for recruitment or job evaluation;
- to provide an organizational overview which will pinpoint duplication or omission of tasks.

The first purpose is the most important, which suggests that the best people to write job descriptions are the job holder and manager working together. If they write the description themselves, they are much more likely to use it on a day-to-day basis as a 'live' tool, and keep it up to date. A large part of the value of the exercise lies also in the discussion necessary to produce the description – it is amazing how often the process of writing a job description brings to light and resolves unacknowledged disagreements about job performance.

Trainers too, acting as job analysts, may write job descriptions, usually after interviewing the job holder and manager concerned. To make sure the jobs are reasonable (managers have been known to propose jobs requiring such vastly different levels of skill that it would be impossible to find them together in one person), consult national competency standards for the job area concerned. These are often based on a framework of typical job functions, for instance, in the training area, identifying training needs. These functions are divided into standard units or activities, arranged in a hierarchy of different job levels. For example, for the training officer job level, identifying training needs might involve gathering information on individual training needs. A training manager might be more concerned with identifying organizational needs.

When it comes to writing the job description, whoever does so, it is important that information is gathered and recorded in a consistent way, and as succinctly as possible. Concentrate throughout on outcomes and results, and how these contribute to the overall purpose of the job. Describe job functions with active not passive verbs – eg 'the job holder runs the following courses', rather than 'the following courses are run', or 'the job holder is responsible for the following courses'.

Equally, make your verbs specific. 'Running' a course, in a document addressed to training staff, seems unlikely to be misunderstood; however, you might want to distinguish between actually presenting training sessions and coordinating other people's sessions in a seminar. Taking some common 'I thought you were doing that' examples, you might also want to make it clear whether 'running' a course includes:

- room set-up;
- checking equipment;
- checking visual aids;
- making available enough sets of handouts etc.

As far as is possible without being too wordy, job descriptions should dispel any potential ambiguity. Numbers help. It is often useful, if not always easy, to allocate an approximate percentage of time spent on each major activity. These percentages are very unlikely to add up to 100 per cent – anything from 60 per cent to 90 per cent may be realistic depending on the nature and level of the job. To take one example, even a machine operator's job has incalculables such as downtime, company or union meetings etc, which could easily account for 10 per cent of the operator's time. Managers, at the other extreme, may find as much as 50 per cent of their time difficult to allocate.

There are many formats for job descriptions. One format which is particularly useful for job holders writing their own descriptions is the job analysis questionnaire. It can also be used by job analysts to structure an interview. As with all questionnaires, make the questions clear and specific, allow enough space for the answers, and keep the document as short as possible. Job analysis questionnaires running to 10 pages are daunting for all concerned.

The job analysis questionnaire may well be sufficient as a job description. However, if the descriptions are to be used frequently for recruitment and job evaluation, a more easily comparable format is helpful. Most organizations have their own preferred approach. One, commendably brief, example had a front sheet which stated the overall purpose of the job, working conditions and required skills; a second page (or the reverse of the sheet) for the major responsibilities and functions of the job.

This format has the advantage that the job responsibilities and functions are listed on a single page, which can be pinned up above the work area as a constant reminder. Job descriptions are notorious for being buried in a bottom drawer, and only dusted off for the yearly performance appraisal, if then. The shorter and more visible they are, the better their chance of being kept up to date.

Performance standards

Job descriptions describe *what* the job does; performance standards identify *how well* it should be done.

As with job descriptions, performance standards are best specified by the job holder and manager working together. Trainers, however, can help by identifying comparable external standards and by providing models for writing standards.

In the UK, nationwide standards are being specified for all occupations, but organizations may well want to adapt these or to specify their own company-specific performance standards.

The UK Training and Development Standards may usefully serve as a general model. The Standards are in three parts:

- An 'element of competence', essentially an activity: 'Select, prepare and adapt exercises and simulations to support collaborative learning'. Note the action verbs: 'select', 'prepare' and 'adapt'. When writing company-specific standards, trainers should match these activities to the job descriptions.
- 'Performance criteria.' These are the core of the standards. They consist of four or five critical outcomes or results for each activity which, taken together, will tell you if the activity is being performed competently: 'Written support materials (existing, adapted and original) are accurate and in a style and format appropriate to the needs and capabilities of the audience'.
- 'Range indicators.' These define the conditions which may qualify the activity, such as available resources, prescribed methods, locations etc. 'Learning materials: written text, graphical, audio, visual display.'

Obviously, national standards are written broadly so as to cover all possible aspects of a job. Companies preparing their own standards might wish to modify the format.

In general terms, all performance standards should *measure competent performance*. These three words bear examination:

Measure. Numbers are the best measurements, of course (eg budget, sales figures, production statistics, course evaluation ratings), as they are less ambiguous than words. For example: 'Average end-of-course ratings should not be less than: achievement of objectives – 5 out of 6; overall rating – 4 out of 6'.

Quantitative measures are not, however, infallible – people can play the numbers game very industriously; nor are they realistically obtainable in all circumstances. How do you measure numerically the success of a relationship? You should also consider whether the criterion is worth measuring – complex control systems monitoring less-than-critical criteria only add to bureaucracy.

Qualitative measures may well be as important as quantitative ones. Unfortunately they are harder to write and, often, to monitor. Write them using specific, concrete language – the fewer the abstractions, the greater the likelihood of common understanding. Examples can be very helpful, provided they are recognized as being just examples, and do not exclude other situations.

For instance, the standard quoted earlier, about written materials being accurate and appropriate to their readers' needs and capabilities, could have as an example: 'If readers may be unfamiliar with any technical, industry, or company terms or abbreviations, these should be defined on the first occasion they are used in a document'.

Competent. What is competent? Do you set standards to measure the 'best practice', or what is generally OK, or what is only barely acceptable? The answer will vary from one company to another. The important point is that manager and job holder should understand the word in the same way.

Performance. Performance is the outcome of a job, the results, not the input (eg the skill or effort required). That *seems* obvious. Consider as a standard: 'Written support materials should be prepared with care and effort'. This standard could be met by materials which were completely unsuitable for their purpose, and some very effective materials may be produced with comparatively little effort. But input criteria may become important (and contentious) when standards are used in performance appraisal. It is human nature to want hard work recognized and rewarded (even if it was unproductive!). In some situations (see the section on competency descriptions below), input criteria can be useful and important; just don't let them creep in without being aware of what you are doing.

One final point to consider with performance standards is that some outcomes are more important than others. If you want to get sophisticated, you can weight your standards – in particular if they are used to determine financial reward.

Performance objectives

Many companies have formal performance measurement systems which embrace both standards and objectives. Whether or not you work to a formal system, both standards and objectives are useful tools for trainers and managers.

Performance standards cover the regular job activities. Objectives refer to one-off tasks, projects and goals, either job-related ('prepare a course to meet managers' needs for negotiation skills'), or for personal development ('improve your negotiation skills'). All the comments made above about measuring competent performance apply equally to performance objectives. The main difference in writing standards and objectives is that objectives need a target date.

Competency descriptions

The word 'competent' has already been frequently used in this chapter – a 'competency' is a skill or behaviour which is essential to achieve competent performance, and it may therefore be seen as an 'input' element to a performance standard or objective. However, in contrast with the earlier 'care and effort' example, required competences are usually restricted to those skills and behaviours whose lack, *however good the measurable performance outcomes*, would detract from the overall performance. For instance, a manager with poor one-to-one coaching skills may achieve excellent results; nevertheless, the lack of this competency will, in the long term, detract from the overall performance. Competency descriptions are frequently used in performance management or appraisal systems, so it is critical to describe the desired behaviour or skill *as clearly as possible*, by using 'action' verbs and examples. Typically these descriptions are expressed as a rating scale, with descriptors 'anchoring' the two ends of the scale, and sometimes intermediate points too. The achieved level of competency is marked on the scale.

Level 4	Level 3	Level 2	Level 1
High		Medium	Low
• Agrees challenging but achievable goals with employee. • Reviews progress with employee. • Always listens to employee, and asks questions to enable employee to derive own solution to problems.		• Sets goals for employee. • Reviews progress with employee. • May listen to employee, but tends to suggest solutions to problems.	• Tells employee what to do.

Figure 5.1 Competency description: one-to-one coaching

6

Procedures, Job Aids and Manuals

Summary

- A company-wide and controlled method of writing procedures will avoid duplication, omission and confusion. Essential elements are standardized procedure layout, standardized reference coding, review and control. Also important are clear objectives, systematic design, and language which is consistent and appropriate to the user.
- Job aids may be considered as mini-procedures. They give brief but detailed information on how to perform a particular function.
- Lengthy procedures, or collections of related procedures, may become training and reference manuals. These need to be laid out and indexed for easy use.

Procedures

I will practise what I am about to preach by setting out guidelines for writing procedures in the form of a procedure (see overleaf).

Job aids

Trainers may also need to write job aids for employees, either to reinforce training in a task or procedure, or following a general analysis of the job. Job aids are more detailed than job descriptions or even procedures, but normally only cover a single task. Their function is to remind the employee of what needs to be done. They therefore have to be written with the employee constantly in mind,

		See also	Rev
1.0	**OBJECTIVE**		
	To provide a guide to writing procedures, covering format, design, style and control.		
2.0	**FORMAT**		
2.1	CONSISTENCY		
	Unlike job aids, procedures should not be produced in different sizes and formats. Their primary purposes are training and reference, rather than acting as on-the-job reminders; a consistent format allows users to track down information easily.	below	
2.2	LEFT-HAND FACING PAGES		
	Procedures should normally be held in binders so that they can be opened flat with both left- and right-hand facing pages visible. Print the procedures only on right-hand pages, and reserve the left-hand ones for reproducing any relevant charts, diagrams, forms etc, which are referred to on that page of the procedures. Photo-reducing these will enable you to add pointers and comments.		
2.3	COLUMNS		
	Use the column on the left for section and subsection numbering, and those on the right for cross-references and highlighting revisions.		

Ref no: A–326–001   Title: WRITING PROCEDURES

Written by: N. Stimson   Date written: 10/90

Approved by: P. Edwards   Date revised: 2/91

Distribution: All managers and supervisors

Ref no: A–326–001   Title: WRITING PROCEDURES

		See also	Rev
2.4	REFERENCE NUMBERING		

Some sort of standard company-wide reference numbering system is necessary for most companies, but keep it as simple as possible and use existing codes which people already know.

The reference for this document, A-326-001, stands for:

A – Administration, a major class of procedures. Other typical categories might be Finance, Production, Marketing etc. These could be denoted either by a letter or number code.

326 – departmental cost code for Training Department.

001 – procedure number, unique within Training Department procedures.

3.0   DESIGN

3.1   OBJECTIVES SECTION

This should tell the reader what the procedure covers, and what any user of the procedure should be able to do.

See also: as in 1.0 above

3.2   DESIGN STEPS

3.2.1   For each operation in the procedure, ask yourself:

What is being done now? **What else might be done?**

Who does it? **Who else might do it?**

Where is it done? **Where else might it be done?**

When is it done? **When else might it be done?**

How is it done? **How else might it be done?**

Ref no: A–326–001	Title: WRITING PROCEDURES		
		See also	Rev
3.2.2	For each operation, identify what information, equipment, materials are necessary for the operation to be performed.		
3.2.3	For each operation, identify and, where appropriate, design the output format.		
3.2.4	Identify clearly, by job title, who performs and who may authorize each operation.		
3.2.5	Sequence the operations, highlighting parallel or alternative operations. Flowcharts are easy to follow and understand.	Ch 18	
3.2.6	Consider the treatment of exceptions. You may want to put these in an appendix rather than in the main procedure.		
3.2.7	Consider whether to repeat information which is held elsewhere or just cross-reference it. Remember that all procedures should be able to stand alone and enable the user to perform the operation.		
3.3	KEY DESIGN CRITERIA Identify clearly any important factors and their impact on the operations. These might include: – legal requirements – safety precautions – security – confidentiality – quality control – audit controls – management – job flexibility. information needs		
4.0	**STYLE**		
4.1	SECTIONS AND PARAGRAPHS As far as possible, give each section or subsection a separate, unique heading.	Ch 3	

Ref no: A–326–001   Title: WRITING PROCEDURES

		See also	Rev
4.1.1	Use consistent text enhancements (capitals, underlining, bold print) to identify them.		
4.1.2	Use a numeric section numbering system, as in this procedure.	Ch 3	
4.1.3	Each process or action should constitute a separate line or paragraph.		
4.2	CHOICE OF WORDS	Ch 2	
4.2.1	Use the imperative or present tense, second person ('you').		
4.2.2	Keep terminology consistent (eg do not refer to both 'billing' and 'invoicing' for the same process). Frequent repetition of the same term is stylistically acceptable.		
4.2.3	Refer to forms, procedures and reports by title and any reference number.		
4.2.4	Choose language appropriate to the user – technical jargon *is* appropriate if the user will understand it.		
5.0	**CONTROL**		
5.1	REVIEW AND APPROVAL		
	All procedures should be reviewed by the user and approved by the immediate supervisor. Procedures which span several areas of operation should be approved at the appropriate level of authority.		
5.2	UPDATING		
5.2.1	Users should notify the procedure writer of any ongoing revisions which are needed.		
5.2.2	The procedure writer should *immediately* revise the procedure to incorporate any		8/01

Ref no: A–326–001	Title: WRITING PROCEDURES		
		See also	Rev
	major changes, eg new equipment, new format of input or output, new or significant changes in activities.		
5.2.3	The procedure writer should review the procedure regularly in order to include any less urgent changes, eg new job titles, minor changes in activities.		
5.2.4	Revised pages should be reissued to all procedure-holders with a covering note indicating the changes; for extensive amendments reissue the whole procedure.		
5.3	CENTRAL MONITORING If the master copies of procedures are held centrally, they can be monitored to: – identify any duplication of activities; – highlight areas where procedures do not exist; – ensure proper approval and authorization; – ensure that they are kept up to date; – check consistency of writing.		

and must take account of his or her previous knowledge, or lack of it. They are particularly useful for critical or infrequent tasks, and are often written as checklists, flowcharts, decision trees or step-by-step instructions. Whatever format is chosen, the following structure is useful to ensure no major points are missed.

1. Preparation. What needs to be known or done before the task can be performed; what information, materials or equipment need to be ready. Diagrams may sometimes be helpful.
2. Start-up. Any preliminaries, including commissioning or setting up equipment.
3. Task. All steps, in order of performance. You normally need to do the task yourself, maybe several times, before writing the instructions. Include only essential details, but enough to enable the task to be completed.
4. Close-down. Finishing procedures, including any decommissioning of equipment, recording of results or reporting to other people.

Language *must* be clearly understood. Avoid elegant sentences: short phrases, each covering a single point, will be followed more easily. If employees' reading ability is limited, use step-by-step diagrams, but express the instructions briefly in words too. And just to make sure the job aid is as foolproof as you think, test it out on typical employees beforehand.

Since job aids exist to help the employee actually perform the task, they should not be filed away in a manual. They are more useful pinned on the wall above the piece of equipment to be operated, or stuck at the front of a record or log book.

The job aid shown in Figure 6.1 could be used by training officers or anyone setting up a course. It could be displayed in the training room or where the course materials are stored.

Presentation is paramount. Job aids which are attached to equipment should be bright, easy-to-read posters, laminated for cleanliness and durability. Even job aids for clerical procedures benefit from being covered in transparent protective material if they are likely to be used frequently. Size may also be important. A5 or credit-card-sized reminders, which fit employees' personal filing systems, are more likely to be carried and referred to regularly.

Manuals

Procedure manuals usually consist of collections of related procedures. It is helpful to include reference aids such as contents pages and indexes.

Contents pages are easy to include and keep up to date. If the procedures are well-established and unlikely to change frequently, it is useful to have sequential page numbering through the whole document; otherwise the page reference has to include the procedure number too.

Indexes are considerably more complicated. Specialist indexing packages exist for those with a great enough need. Alternatively, indexes can be created manually, by scanning each page and picking out the main points. This is tedious and time-consuming, although the chore can be reduced by using word processors to find key words.

Updating indexes is also a major job. You not only have to include references to the changed elements of the procedures, but inserted passages may also have caused page numbering changes. This is where separate page numbering for each procedure is valuable, otherwise you may need to renumber all the pages of subsequent procedures. In any case, it is often necessary to recreate the index completely each time there are changes, so, if you are not using a specialist package, it is sensible to restrict indexes, where possible, to the well-established procedures.

TRAINING COURSE SET-UP

If possible set up the training room the night before a course.
CHECK:

- **arrangement of furniture** → ACCORDING TO PLAN

- **placing of equipment** → CAN EVERYONE SEE EVERYTHING?

- **safety and security** → UNPLUG / SWITCH OFF ELECTRICITY
  → CHECK NO TRAILING LEADS
  → LOCK TRAINING ROOM OVERNIGHT

- **equipment back-up**
  - □ spare bulbs
  - □ fuses

- **participant materials**
  - □ nameplates
  - □ handouts
  - □ pads
  - □ manuals
  - □ pencils

- **standard materials**
  - □ flip chart pads
  - □ sticky gum
  - □ hole punch
  - □ flip chart pens
  - □ adhesive tape
  - □ stapler
  - □ sticky dots
  - □ paper clips

- **trainer materials**
  - □ visuals
  - □ course notes
  - □ props

- **refreshments**

Figure 6.1 Job aid

7

Forms and Questionnaires

Summary

Forms and questionnaires are often difficult to design as they have multiple users – the people who fill in the information and those who interpret it. KISS is the key issue; attractive layout is also extremely important. This chapter considers:

- forms;
- simple questionnaires;
- attitude surveys;
- tests.

Forms

Trainers may need to design forms for various purposes, both for their own use and for that of one or more other people. It is therefore critical to identify the most important reader or user of the form. For instance, with a job application form, is it the applicant or the recruiter? Surely the applicant, but most application forms are designed for organizational convenience.

Taking a performance appraisal form as another example, is the most important user:

- the manager who completes the report?
- the employee who receives a copy?
- the 'grandfather' manager or other organizational watchdog?
- the training officer who extracts training needs?
- the HR professional who translates performance ratings into salary figures?

Depending on the scheme, it could be any of them, although most schemes would *say* it was the employee. This is often not reflected in the forms, which may be heavy on demographic information (division, department, region, grade, length of service, age, job history etc), and consist of a formidable array of performance rating boxes with little or no room for comments.

So, establishing the prime user and his or her needs is the necessary starting point. Keeping it as short and simple as possible (KISS) is a need *all* users share, but one which is often sacrificed in the inevitably doomed attempt to satisfy everyone. Ruthless pruning is normally the best policy, if necessary creating two simple forms for different users rather than one complex one.

Let us consider a few important elements of forms design and see how they are illustrated in a performance appraisal form.

Boxes should be large enough for manual or keyboard completion and there should be enough space for comments. Typewriters or word processors may not allow enough flexibility of layout for forms design – if the form will be in frequent use, it is worth having it printed or using a specialized computer forms package.

If completion instructions are necessary, they should be on the form itself. A smaller typeface is usually acceptable for these, provided that it can still be read when photocopied or faxed.

If the form includes ratings, beware of the common 'central tendency' – picking the middle-of-the-road option every time. Having an even number of ratings (four or six, rather than five) reduces this. Incidentally, no matter how many rating options you offer, some people will nevertheless put their mark between the boxes, so you do need to consider how you will interpret that.

Designing Web forms requires specialist expertise, and computer packages exist to assist in this. However, the same basic design principles should apply. (See also Chapter 13.)

Questionnaires

These are used and often designed by trainers for various purposes. Common examples are a simple training needs survey, a job analysis questionnaire or an end-of-course rating sheet. Such questionnaires as these are fairly straightforward to design, even where they contain rating scales.

More specialized questionnaires may be needed for attitude surveys or to identify skills and abilities. Whilst these are not necessarily difficult to devise, interpretation is critical and the design of the questionnaire can affect the results. Major surveys or ability tests should be left to specialists, but you may want to prepare smaller-scale ones yourself.

PERFORMANCE APPRAISAL

EXPLANATION OF RATINGS

Not meeting basic job requirements: This does not necessarily imply poor employee performance – it may result from other factors eg postponing certain major activities because of changing priorities.

Meeting job requirements: This indicates consistently satisfactory performance of all major job areas.

Exceeding job requirements: This should be used when the whole job is being consistently performed at a fully satisfactory level, and some important areas at a significantly higher level.

Outstanding: This indicates exceptional performance.

Ratings should be amplified with comments as appropriate

OVERALL RATING OF PERFORMANCE

Not meeting basic requirements	Meeting job requirements	Exceeding job requirements	Outstanding

COMMENTS

Figure 7.1 Performance appraisal form

EVALUATION QUESTIONNAIRE FOR SESSION CONTENT AND TRAINER

Weigh the two statements and decide where along the scale 6-5-4-3-2-1 the most accurate description lies.

6   STRONGLY AGREE with the statement on the LEFT   2   SOMEWHAT AGREE with the statement on the RIGHT
5   SOMEWHAT AGREE with the statement on the LEFT   1   STRONGLY AGREE with the statement on the RIGHT
                    4 or 3   Neither statement alone is accurate – answer lies somewhere in the middle

CIRCLE the number that best described your thought. If a statement does not apply, leave it blank.

EXAMPLE:
c)   I learnt something new   6-5-4-3-2-1   c)   I learnt nothing new
k)   The room was ideal for this session   6-5-4-3-2-1   k)   The room was inadequate

a) Subject of session directly related to my needs	6-5-4-3-2-1	a) I have no need for the subject offered
b) The objective of the session was met	6-5-4-3-2-1	b) The objective was not met
c) I learnt something new	6-5-4-3-2-1	c) I learnt nothing new
d) The session covered the right amount of material	6-5-4-3-2-1	d) The session covered too much/too little* material
e) Session material was well-organized	6-5-4-3-2-1	e) Topics seemed out of order
f) Explanations were clear and simple	6-5-4-3-2-1	f) Explanations were unclear and confusing
g) The session was alive and interesting	6-5-4-3-2-1	g) The session was dull
h) Reading material was outstanding	6-5-4-3-2-1	h) Reading material was poor
i) Exercises were helpful and stimulating	6-5-4-3-2-1	i) Exercises were not helpful
j) Visual aids were outstanding	6-5-4-3-2-1	j) Visual aids were poor/not used*
k) The room was ideal for this session	6-5-4-3-2-1	k) The room was inadequate
l) Overall the session was outstanding	6-5-4-3-2-1	l) The session was worthless

* Delete as appropriate

Figure 7.2 End-of-course rating sheet

Attitude surveys

When you design an attitude survey, bear the following points in mind.

Since completion is often voluntary, the survey *must be attractive and easy to complete*. Unclear instructions, too many questions, fuzzy printing, asking for demographic information which will identify individual respondents – all these are likely to reduce your completion rate significantly. Spelling out the purpose of the survey, and how and when you will tell respondents of the results, will make people take it seriously.

You are likely to be the person collating and interpreting the results, so make it as easy as possible. If the analysis is to be done manually, avoid as much calculation as you can. If you will be using a computer package, such as a simple spreadsheet, consider in advance how you will lay out the information, how it needs to be sorted, and what combination of factors you will use for analysis. You may want to seek the help of the computer department. The attitude survey in Figure 7.3 was in large part analysed manually. Points were allotted to each response (fully agree +2, partly agree +1, partly disagree -1, fully disagree -2), and these multiplied by the importance rating (1, 2 or 3). A number of questions covered the same main topics, eg motivation, efficiency, quality-consciousness. The replies were analysed both on an individual question basis and according to topic. With about 200 replies, this was tedious but possible. With more, it would have been impossible. Even so, only limited demographic analyses could be managed, eg by region or category of staff.

Wherever you can, express questions positively. This is easier to understand than a tangle of double negatives.

You will get a more accurate picture if 'right' answers do not always have the same rating; otherwise respondents will get into the habit of answering, say, 5 or 6, and will not think about each question. It is better for the 'right' answer to be 6 for one question and 1 for the next. However, this does make manual collation of results considerably more difficult, which is why the example end-of-course rating sheet and employee opinion questionnaire both disregard this principle.

If possible, use a weighting factor so that respondents can identify how important they consider a factor as well as how they rate it. Although this makes manual collation of results more difficult it has advantages. In the case of this employee opinion questionnaire it was well worth doing, as the importance ratings changed the overall picture significantly.

Decide in advance how you will deal with incorrectly-completed question-naires. It is common for people to give ratings between boxes, or even beyond the end of a scale.

EMPLOYEE OPINION QUESTIONNAIRE

Please read each item below. Tick the extent to which you agree or disagree with the statement made and circle the importance rating that you give to the item. Your response should reflect your view of the company overall, not just your own situation.

	Agree		Disagree		Importance (Scale: 1–low 3-high)		
	Fully	Partly	Partly	Fully			
1. Morale is high	[]	[]	[]	[]	1	2	3
2. Managers use their time well	[]	[]	[]	[]	1	2	3
3. When mistakes are made, we try to learn from them	[]	[]	[]	[]	1	2	3
4. Staff are usually involved in decisions which affect their work	[]	[]	[]	[]	1	2	3
5. In our company, quality is of the highest importance	[]	[]	[]	[]	1	2	3

Figure 7.3 Start of an attitude survey

Test the questionnaire for ease of completion and interpretation before printing and issuing it. If it is confidential, test it on someone outside your company.

Be cautious in interpreting the results, especially of a one-off survey. People may be wary of what is expected of them, and say what they think you want to hear rather than what they really think. Repeat surveys, highlighting any changes in attitude, are usually more valid.

Publish the results, whatever they are. Secrecy destroys trust.

Tests

The aim with most test questionnaires is not to pass or fail the people taking the test, but to provide information about them and their level of knowledge or aptitude in certain areas.

Tests of knowledge are comparatively straightforward to prepare. Different types of questions will establish different degrees of knowledge. Multiple choice, matching or true/false questions are good for discrimination and simple relationships:

'Which is the correct spelling?   questionaire / questionnair / questionnaire'

Essay questions will identify depth of understanding, but are slower and more difficult to assess.

'To what extent. . .'
'Compare and contrast. . .'
'Examine the effects of. . .'

Knowledge tests are better if they are short and selective than if they try to be comprehensive. Make sure that the questions are clear (test all tests before using them), and that they cover the most important and most commonly-needed areas, not the most abstruse ones. Formulation of questions is covered in more detail in Chapter 11.

Psychological tests are not for amateurs to design or use, and some 'communication skills' or 'leadership style' questionnaires are similar in sensitivity. Many such instruments are available commercially. Their validity varies and interpretation of results should be handled with caution.

You may be tempted to customize them for your own organization, but don't. It is a breach of copyright (unless permission is received) and destroys whatever validity the test has. If you need a serious test specific to your own organization, get it designed by experts, but remember that, for any reliable interpretation of results, it would need to be validated with a sample population. This can take a long time.

There is no reason, however, why you should not design your own light-hearted quizzes. Whilst these would not pretend to be a scientific measure, they can still give valuable insights into behaviour or skills. Make them fun and quick to complete, and do not forget that they are at best only indicators.

	Always	Often	Fairly often	Less often	Rarely	Never
How often do you:						
• identify your reader's needs and attitudes before you start writing?	☐	☐	☐	☐	☐	☐
• write down your objective before you start writing?	☐	☐	☐	☐	☐	☐
• write down some sort of plan or structure before you start writing?	☐	☐	☐	☐	☐	☐
• consciously choose simple words?	☐	☐	☐	☐	☐	☐
• check your FOG Index?	☐	☐	☐	☐	☐	☐
• plan the visual presentation of your writing?	☐	☐	☐	☐	☐	☐
• get someone else to review your writing?	☐	☐	☐	☐	☐	☐

Score: 5 for each **Always**; 4 for each **Often**; 3 for each **Fairly often**;
2 for each **Less often**; 1 for each **Rarely**; 0 for each **Never**.

If you scored:
31–35   Wonderful! (Who am I to cast doubts on your veracity?)
21–30   Very good. I hope your writing generally meets with the approval and success it deserves.
11–20   I expect most people will fall into this category. Why not use this quiz as a writing checklist and push up your score?
5–10   It really is worth trying out these tips. You will find your writing much more likely to achieve what you want.
0–4   Oh dear! I *am* glad you bought this book.

Figure 7.4 Writing skills quiz

8

Course Notes

Summary

This chapter covers:

- Joining instructions. These should be short, welcoming in tone, and include all administrative details and any pre-course work or checklists.
- Trainer's notes, often called a lesson or teaching plan. These may be on paper or cue-cards. A useful method is to use a standard 4-column approach, with columns for time, content, exercises, audiovisual aids. Many PC-based presentation packages have the facility to add notes pages.
- The trainer's review of the course. This should allow easy reference and follow-up.

Joining instructions

Joining instructions are often a trainer's first contact with course participants – they strongly influence the expectations for the course and therefore its ultimate success.

The instructions should take the form of a short (approximately one page) memo or letter sent before the event to all participants, advising them where and when the course will be held.

The formality of the word 'instructions' rather belies their purpose, which is to welcome participants and reinforce their desire to benefit from the course. Depending on the participants and the course itself, this may be done by allaying anxieties, detailing individual and company benefits, or pointing out an urgent need.

Other purposes of the joining instructions include helping participants gain the most benefit from the course, by suggesting pre-course assignments, checklists, and briefing sessions with participants' managers or course tutors. Also, obviously, timetables and administrative arrangements should be made clear, including a map if the venue is difficult to find. These may be covered in separate attachments to the memo or letter.

Trainer's notes

The purpose of these is to enable the trainer to run the course.

This is not a book on how to prepare a training course, so it would not be appropriate to go into detail about training objectives, course structure, different training techniques etc. As a quick reminder, however:

1. Write behavioural training objectives. The UK National Standards for Training and Development stress that 'learning objectives [should be] derived from an appropriate and relevant analysis of the requirements of the role'.

    For a presentation skills course you might write:
    'Participants will (a useful introduction as it forces you to identify the behaviour change, and express it as a verb):
    –   identify the needs of their audience;
    –   identify the objective of their presentation to meet those needs;
    –   identify how to test that the objective has been met;
    –   plan and structure their presentation to meet their objective. . .'

2. Work out how to test that these objectives have been achieved, and write the test (even if you do not plan to administer it in that form) eg writing objectives, analysing a lesson plan, giving presentations.

3. Next identify what information participants must know to complete the test (and, if you wish, 'should know' and 'nice to know' elements) eg how to write a behavioural objective, verbs to use and avoid, etc.

4. Start the presentation by arousing interest. (Explaining the course objectives and describing what you will cover may be less entertaining than a brilliant multimedia demonstration or witty jokes, but the straightforward approach often works just as well.)

5. Break the ice quickly, by getting participants talking and doing things, eg the paired introductions exercise in the lesson plan below.

6. Structure 'must know' items (and any others you decide to include) from the *student's* perspective.

7.   Summarize frequently.
8.   Make obvious the links between different topics eg using the introductions exercise as a presentation model, as in the lesson plan below.
9.   Select the techniques and audiovisual aids which will best reinforce each training point. (See Chapter 9.)
10. End on a high note and emphasize the links back to the work situation, eg by making the final exercise of a presentations skills course a 'real life' one – a presentation which the participants will really have to give.

Many trainers have their own preferred way of setting out their notes but, whatever the format, the following information should be included:

- the basic content which is being covered and the methods used (eg lecture, question-and-answer etc);
- links between the content and any audiovisual aids, handouts and exercises;
- time checks along the way.

Initially this information may be written in some detail as a lesson or teaching plan, which can be preserved for other trainers. Points to consider include:

- Objective, equipment and materials information should be found on the first sheet only, not on continuation sheets.
- Timings can be estimated either as actual times, as shown in Figure 8.1, or elapsed time from the beginning of the session (or both – use colour to distinguish between them).
- The content column can be as explicit or as cryptic as you wish. (However, it should not be so cryptic that other trainers cannot use the notes. Emergencies do happen.) Highlighting in different colours lecture portions, questions, desired answers and activities gives a useful overview of the anticipated dynamics of the course, and indicates where any time savings can be made.
- Handouts are often associated with exercises, so may be referred to in that column. It is useful to give them an identifying letter or number.
- Similarly, number overhead transparencies to avoid confusion.

If you wish, the material can be abbreviated on to:

- Cue cards.
- Overhead transparency frames.
- A single piece of cardboard (eg the back of an A4 pad). This serves as a complete one-day-at-a-glance route map of the course, and is also useful

```
┌─────────────────────────────────────────────────────────────────────────┐
│                              LESSON PLAN                                  │
│                                                                           │
│   Title:      Presentation Skills for Managers              Date:  9/01   │
│                                                                           │
│   Objective:  Participants will develop their presentation skills and employ good │
│               preparation and presentation techniques.                    │
│   Equipment:  Overhead projector; laptop; multimedia (LCD) projector; slide projector; │
│               flip chart; video recorder (VHS); TV.                       │
│   Materials:  25 overhead transparencies (Tr1–25); 32 35mm slides (Sl 1–32); │
│               12 handouts (A–L); video.                                   │
└─────────────────────────────────────────────────────────────────────────┘
```

Time	Content	Exercises	A-V aids
9.00	Welcome. Introduce self. Course arrangements.		Tr 1
9.05	Participants to exchange information in pairs and introduce neighbour.	Pair ex	
9.25	Use 'introductions' exercise as presentation model. 4 focuses: audience / objective / information / presentation		Flip ch
9.30	Presentation only tip of iceberg.		Tr 2

Figure 8.1 Trainer's lesson plan for start of Presentation Skills course

for systematically concealing/revealing information on overhead transparencies. (Incidentally, cardboard is better than paper for this purpose, as it is not blown off by the overhead projector fan. However, it has the disadvantage that the trainer cannot see the concealed material through it.)

Lesson plans (either full or abbreviated) can also be written in the Notes pages on presentation packages like Microsoft PowerPoint. These packages are extremely useful, and have transformed the general standard of presentations in the last few years, but they are structured around slides, and therefore there is a tendency to overuse these audiovisual aids. The packages are best used by:

● Firstly, considering the overall structure of the presentation or course, in terms of major content elements.
● Next, identifying which type of presentation method, activity or audio-visual aid will best reinforce or illustrate the message of each element.

PRESENTATION SKILLS FOR MANAGERS		①	
TIME	CONTENT	EX	A-V
9.00	WELCOME PAIRED INTROS	PAIRS	1
9.25	USE INTROS AS PRES. MODEL 4 FOCUSES		F/C
9.30	ICEBERG		2

Figure 8.2 Trainer's cue–card for start of Presentation Skills course

- Only then starting to use the presentation package. Include the appropriate lesson plan portion in the notes pages for each slide. Material which is reinforced or illustrated by methods or audiovisual aids other than slides should be included in the notes page for the preceding slide.

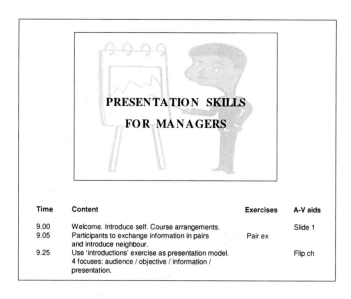

Figure 8.3 PowerPoint notes page for first slide of Presentation Skills course

Trainer's review of the course

Most trainers evaluate for themselves the success or otherwise of a course or other learning event. Systematically recording these evaluations has a number of benefits:

- Preparing statistical analyses of training becomes a much simpler task.
- Necessary actions or changes to the course or learning event are less likely to be left to the last minute, or even forgotten.
- Other trainers can appreciate how the course or learning event has developed, and anticipate the likely expectations and reactions of participants.

The following headings may be helpful in structuring the information:

- name and date of course;
- trainer;
- list of participants;
- administration;
- venue;
- course content;
- participant reactions;
- average participant ratings;
- follow-up.

A 'who and when' action column is particularly useful for following-up and ensuring that the actions really happen.

9

Course Visuals

Summary

- When producing visuals, KISS and PUP are more than guidelines – they become rules.
- A third rule is to use colour, both to enliven the visual and to emphasize particular points.
- Overhead transparencies are very commonly used visuals; they are a very flexible medium, comparatively easy to prepare, and provide ready-made session handouts. Special materials and the use of computer graphics increase the professional effect, whilst overlay techniques hold the audience's attention as the message builds up.
- PC-controlled slide shows are increasingly frequently used, adding significantly to the professionalism of overhead transparencies by the inclusion of animation and multimedia displays.
- Use of 35mm slides is decreasing, but they are still a valuable alternative resource. The principles for preparing 35mm slides are similar to those for overhead transparencies. The medium, though less flexible than the overhead projector, can give a more dramatic and professional impression – qualities which should be exploited both in the visual presentation and the accompanying narrative.
- Other common visual aids include flipcharts and posters.

Rule 1 – KISS

We have established the importance of keeping text short and simple. Now let us look at some specific points.

VERTICAL VISUALS	HORIZONTAL VISUALS
Four words at most	Six or fewer words per line
Four words at most	Six or fewer words per line
Four words at most	Four or fewer lines per visual
Six lines at most	Four or fewer lines per visual
Six lines at most	
Six lines at most	

Figure 9.1 How short is short?

This is an ideal. Nobody keeps to it all the time, but it is amazing how much information can be condensed into 24 words.

Incidentally, a comment on lettering. Figure 9.2 shows a visual presented in capital letters. Some people like this, as it makes the visual look more regular and uniform. Others maintain that a mixture of upper and lower case letters (as in normal print) is easier to read and understand, especially if complete sentences feature, eg when a definition is shown. Compare Figure 9.2 with Figure 9.3 – which do you prefer?

Two other issues are raised by these visuals. First, the benefits of using bullet points. These attract your audience's attention and make the points easier to absorb and remember. If the order of the points is important, number them

WHY WRITE?

- PERMANENT RECORD
- FORMALITY
- CONVEYS 'SAME' MESSAGE TO MANY PEOPLE
- CHEAP
- CONTROL OF TIMING
- **TO BE READ**

Figure 9.2 Visual with upper case lettering

instead. Second, the use of a box or border to enclose your words, which also focuses the audience's attention.

Why Write?

- permanent record

- formality

- conveys 'same' message to many people

- cheap

- control of timing

- to be read

Figure 9.3 Visual with lower case lettering

Rule 2 – PUP

You can, of course, avoid the upper and lower case dilemma completely by using pictures rather than words. There are many sources of ready-made pictures:

- Posters and photographs.
- Photographic material stored on the Web.
- Computer graphics packages, which often have a gallery of standard drawings, including drawings of people and of common objects, and maps, cartoons and symbols. These are a tremendous help in producing sophisticated effects simply.
- Volumes of line drawings and cartoons on which copyright has been waived. These are readily available and, as with the computer clip-art galleries, an excellent source of ideas, as well as of the pictures themselves.
- And you can even draw the pictures yourself. You do not need to be a Rembrandt! Stick men cartoons can be very effective.

The following graphics could be computer produced, or drawn by hand (however limited your artistic talent!). As an overhead transparency, this could be built up by overlaying the three responses in turn.

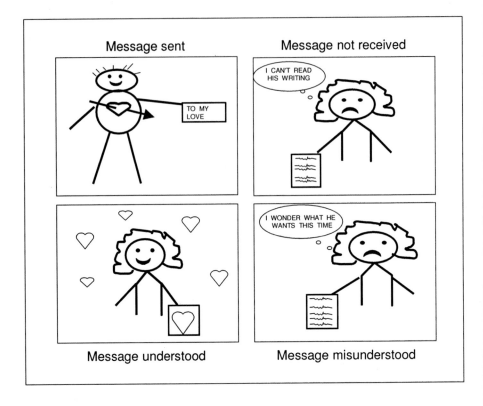

Figure 9.4 Cartoon graphics illustrating successful and unsuccessful communications

Rule 3 – Use colour

Colour is a tool which strengthens visuals enormously, and with the vast palette of colours available in computer graphics packages, your imagination is your only constraint. Be careful, however – colour is only a tool, and an overly-dazzling effect can actually distract people from your message.

Colour can also be used to emphasize or even make points for you, without you needing to spell them out. For instance, if you are gathering ideas at the flip chart, different colours will enable you to classify them as you go, into, say, advantages and disadvantages.

Be aware, however, of the pitfall of colour-blindness. One in twelve males cannot distinguish clearly between red and green.

Overhead transparencies

Many trainers' favourite medium, overhead transparencies are convenient, quick and easy to prepare. Therein lie both their advantages and their, very considerable, disadvantages. It is all too tempting to pile masses of information (instructions and procedures, forms, tables of numbers etc) onto a single transparency, and use it almost as a lesson plan to take you through a 15-minute 'lecturette' – tempting but disastrous.

It is so easy to produce a transparency from any document, simply by photocopying or printing onto an acetate foil, that you can forget that this may not meet the audience's needs. Written documents are primarily meant for individual study at the reader's own pace; overhead transparencies illustrate and emphasize points made at the trainer's or the group's pace. To control this pace, only key words or small amounts of information should be shown at any time. Procedures, forms, charts and tables of numbers all need to be broken down into smaller units which are presented separately. I must admit that I do not always stick to the 24-word maximum I have suggested above, but I do try to use it as a guide.

Small units can sometimes be built up using overlay techniques to give the complete information. Otherwise, if you have to present an overall visual impression of the whole document, do so at the end or just hand it out.

Do not, however, go to the other extreme and have a few words or a small picture lost in acres of empty space in the middle of your transparency – unless, of course, you are trying to achieve a particular effect. As a general rule, try to fill the screen.

Always use large, bold lettering for overhead transparencies. There are several lettering systems ranging from computer-produced fonts to manual techniques such as dry transfer or stencils. Even freehand lettering can look neat and professional if squared paper is used underneath as a guide.

Colour adds enormously to the impact of an overhead transparency, and computer packages can deliver an array of colours, both for the lettering and the background, not to mention any borders or pictures you have included. And there are also, of course, coloured pens for highlighting or freehand work.

Overhead transparencies make convenient handouts too – simply photocopy the original used to produce the transparency.

PC slides

Slides produced by a PC presentation package may be printed onto acetate foils and used as overhead transparencies, or may be projected directly from the PC.

They may also, for portability, be downloaded onto a computer disc or CD and projected via a multimedia or LCD projector. PC-based presentations offer you a variety of additional techniques. However, do take care not to overdo the special effects. In moderation, they can add enormously to the professionalism of the visuals, but too many effects will just confuse people! Animation and multimedia effects also tend to take up large amounts of computer memory, which may make them difficult to send via e-mail or to download onto disc.

Animation

Transition techniques when moving from one slide to the next (fading in the next slide from whatever direction and at whatever speed you choose) create a smooth and polished effect, and varying the transition effect can add emphasis to a particular slide. Animation can also be very effectively used when adding material to a base slide, in much the same way as overlay techniques with overhead transparencies. You can make your text bullets 'fly in' (normally from left to right, but right to left can be used for additional emphasis) and, similarly, overlay additions to charts and pictures.

Sound effects

Music, sound effects from a sound gallery, or voice narration can also be added to PC slide presentations, as can video clips. Do take care that these will actually enhance your presentation – they can all too often become distractions. Full-scale multimedia presentations are not considered here, as they are beyond the scope of this book.

35mm slides

These are used less frequently than in the past, because most of their benefits can now be delivered by PC presentations. Most of the points made above apply equally to 35mm slides. Here are a few other ideas to bear in mind:

● As the room is normally darkened, subtler colour contrasts can be used than with overhead transparencies or PC presentations, and reverse-image techniques (white or a pale colour on a dark background) are particularly powerful.

- Photographs can work very well, especially if interspersed with other graphics.
- Overlay techniques can be simulated by using a sequence of successively more complete slides, building up to the whole.

Slides are potentially a very dramatic medium. To exploit this, the narrative needs to be carefully and vividly scripted in spoken rather than written language – say it aloud to see how it sounds. Timing and pacing also make a great difference to the impact. Do not show a slide and talk about it for half a minute, then show the next and talk about that for half a minute, then show the next... Whilst an average of about half a minute's narrative per slide is about right, you may want to talk about one slide for three or four minutes, and then flip through the next six without saying anything.

I use Figure 9.5 in a short 35mm slide presentation on the use of visual aids. It makes these points:

- The ostensible message about visibility.
- The greater impact of the reverse-image presentation.
- The obvious importance of checking and proofreading.
- The uncomfortable fact that, the more professional the medium, the more glaring any error appears. The same spelling mistake, written on a flipchart in class, could be passed over with a joking correction. This cannot be done with a 35mm slide.

Not bad for four words.

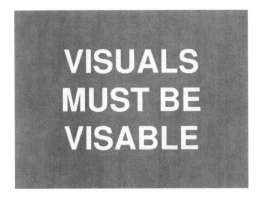

Figure 9.5 A 35mm slide

Other visual aids

The main function of flip charts, whiteboards and blackboards is to allow the trainer to produce instant visual aids during the session. Flip charts can also be used for ready-prepared material. Writing *must* be legible, and it is harder to write neatly on boards than on a flip chart. Squared flip chart paper is a boon.

Posters are often the focal point for a lecture or discussion. They therefore need to be strong in design to keep the audience's attention. Remember the rules about simplicity, pictures and colour. Posters are excellent for anything you want to keep up as a permanent reminder. They are also particularly suitable for mapping a process which you will be discussing in your training session. Incidentally, with a complex process chart, you may want to cover up some parts initially, and reveal them progressively as the session develops.

Preparing posters *can* be very time-consuming. But it need not be. The quickest way I know is to take an A4 master (for example, one prepared for an overhead transparency) and enlarge it to A3 or A2 size. You can then stick this onto coloured card to provide a frame. Very easy, very effective, and very cheap. And, as a final word, look after your posters. They are generally less durable than other visual aids, and so it makes sense to laminate them with clear plastic film, and arrange for protective storage.

10

Course Handouts

Summary

Trainers can:

- Produce full handout materials themselves.
- Let students take their own notes.
- Adopt a combination approach.

All these options have advantages and disadvantages, but the combination approach usually works best. An easy way to create such handouts is to base them on copies of the visuals, with space alongside or on the opposite page for student notes.

Ready-made handouts

After the excitement of thinking through and preparing the course content, many trainers find handouts boring to write. It is hardly surprising, therefore, that many students find them boring to read, and frequently do not bother to do so. To avoid having this happen to your handouts:

- Remember KISS. Only include necessary information, for your students' sake and for your own; structure the information so that students can use and refer to it easily; do not forget the headings; write short paragraphs, short sentences, short words; use a lively, direct style.
- Remember PUP. Pictures, including charts, line drawings or photographs (just make sure they can be clearly reproduced) enliven and clarify text. They should not be add-ons, but an integral and fundamental part of the handout.

- Use acronyms (eg KISS and PUP) to help students remember key points.
- Use layout to attract and retain attention.
- Consider using other formats than A4 sheets, eg A5 checklists for personal filing systems, reminder cards which fit into a diary or pocket, laminated posters to stick above the workplace. Your aim is not a row of glossy training manuals sitting on the shelf, unopened and unread.

Advantages of trainer-produced handouts are:

- You can make sure that they are complete and accurate.
- Students can spend their training time learning, rather than just noting down your words.

Disadvantages are:

- Participants may 'switch off' and concentrate less, when they know there is a handout covering the topic.
- Given that individual students inevitably have different needs, none of the information you provide will be useful for everybody. Finding relevant needles in a pile of hay is rarely worth much effort – and that is what it may feel like to the student. This is the biggest reason why training handouts are largely ignored back on the job.
- It is difficult to find the right time to distribute handouts:

Before the event. Some people may read them in advance, but others (usually the less able or knowledgeable) will not, causing even greater disparity in students' starting knowledge. Also, some people may actually see the handout as a substitute for the training session and not attend at all.

During the session. The temptation is to read them at that stage instead of concentrating on the presentation.

After the event. This is when you are most likely to have students file-and-forget them.

Do-it-yourself

This is the reverse of having the trainer provide ready-made handouts.

The big advantage of having students take their own notes is not that it saves you time and effort (although, of course, it does), but that the notes are more personal to the student and may consequently be better used after the training.

The main disadvantage is that the student who is busy scribbling has the time neither to listen, nor to think, nor to ask questions – a total waste of face-to-face training. Also the notes may be incomplete. This is not always a problem: indeed it is an advantage, if the exclusions are deliberate omissions of less relevant points. But they are more likely to occur because of chance, lack of concentration, or the difficulty of writing at speaking-speed.

Combination approach

Here the trainer provides an outline of the main points covered, with space for the students to amplify as they please.

The outlines should be more than just topic headings. Set out important rules and checklists in full. Use diagrams and pictures to clarify the material and aid retention. Either include all necessary reference material or make sure the students can get hold of it easily. And invite the students to note examples from their own experience to which the training points might be applied. However, do beware of putting in so much information that the outline becomes (and is treated as) trainer-produced notes.

If you use overhead transparencies, slides or prepared flip chart sheets to reinforce your main training points, you can include copies of these in the outline. One easy approach is to have a photocopy of the visuals on the left-hand pages, with space for additional notes on the facing right-hand pages. These right-hand pages should consist of the outline guide with sufficiently large gaps for the students' comments. In an emergency, however, they can be left blank, with the visual copies then providing the total trainer input to the handout. This is similar to the 'handout' pages provided by PC presentation packages.

If you are using a combination approach, you need to pay particular attention to format and presentation. You will add considerably to the professional image if you have a box or border on your pages.

Workbooks (bound or stapled) or loose-leaf folders are more practical than loose sheets stapled together. Not only are they less likely to get lost, but they can be opened flat to let the student see both left- and right-hand pages. You may also want to include any exercises or case study briefings in the workbooks rather than handing them out separately. This certainly looks tidier, but do consider very carefully how the exercise will be performed. With some exercises, it would be extremely awkward to have to carry a workbook or training manual. With others you may not want the participants reading the exercise before you get to it.

In general, the combined approach tries to provide the best of both worlds – the completeness and accuracy of trainer-produced notes, made more relevant and personal by the student's involvement. Its biggest disadvantage is that it may restrict the flexibility of the training session. Students will expect the trainer to cover all the points in the workbook in order, whereas, for that particular group, the trainer may wish to reverse the order or concentrate on some aspects rather than others. You can still do this, of course, provided that you explain to the students when you are deviating, and that you know your workbook well enough to direct them to the right page.

Figure 10.1 Combination approach course manual

11

Course Exercises

Summary

Exercises need as much preparation as any other part of the training course. There are five main stages in preparing all exercises:

1. Identify exercise objective.
2. Outline problem.
3. Devise solution.
4. Prepare instructions for student and trainer.
5. Dry-run.

Major types of exercises include:

- case studies;
- role plays;
- games;
- mazes;
- in-basket exercises.

Are exercises the easy option?

An exercise can seem an easy, not to say lazy, way of filling a slack half-hour or more on a training course – set the participants a problem, the more open-ended the better, and let them get on with it – minimal preparation and a welcome breathing space for the trainer. Ideal, one might think, but the reality is very different. Exercises often take more preparation than any other part of the teaching plan, and the success of the outcome may depend on how carefully they are written. Running the exercise, too, may be very taxing for the trainer.

Like all forms of student involvement, exercises can have unexpected results. We have all experienced the role play that goes awry, or the pre-course test that suggests that the students already know as much as the trainer! But even if they are not always an easy option, exercises are a very valuable one – they create participation and increase learning dramatically.

The same principles apply whatever kind of exercise you are writing. The basic approach has five stages.

Identify objective

What teaching points is the exercise intended to make? What kind of learning is sought:

- memorization (of facts or processes)?
- understanding (of principles and situations)?
- performance (of actions)?

Outline problem

There are two elements here: choosing a question, example or situation, and describing it.

The example should be one familiar to all participants, and the choice should therefore be determined by what you know of the participants.

Describing the problem is the core of the exercise. Consider carefully how much information to include – too little, and the students have to make assumptions, which increases the number of possible solutions; too much, and either the example becomes so complex that students get confused, or the solution becomes too obvious and easy. However, it is worth bearing in mind that what may seem too much information from your point of view, as creator of the exercise, may be too little for the student who comes to it cold.

Devise solution

Where there is a single correct solution, explain it as simply as possible and, if helpful, the method of reaching it.

Where there is no 'right' answer, say so and offer a 'suggested' solution, possibly identifying where this falls short of the ideal. You may want to offer alternative solutions, emphasizing their comparative good and bad points, but take care not to over-complicate the exercise.

Even if the solution will not be handed out to the students, it should still be written. This ensures consistency when different trainers run the exercise.

Prepare instructions

Prepare instructions both for the student, on how to complete the exercise, and for the trainer, on how to run it. They must be clear and straightforward.

The trainer's instructions should be detailed enough to allow another trainer to run the exercise with minimal rehearsal. A standard format trainer's guide is useful to ensure that nothing essential is forgotten.

Dry-run exercise

This is essential. The closer the test group is to the target group the better, but even if that is impossible, dry run the exercise on someone. It is amazing how often an exercise which looks perfectly reasonable on paper just does not work in practice. You are testing:

TRAINER'S GUIDE TO EXERCISE

Exercise: Course:

Format: Indiv / Pairs / Trios / Small gps / Whole gp

Duration: Location:

Other materials/
equipment required:

Primary objective:

Other objectives:

Preparation:

Running the exercise:

Potential problems:

Figure 11.1 Trainer's Guide

- how well the exercise achieves its objective;
- how easily the student can follow your instructions;
- how easily the student can complete the exercise;
- how good the solution is;
- the completeness of the trainer's guide;
- the timing of the exercise, and possibly the location.

Types of exercises

Case studies

A case study is a description of a real or realistic situation which the students have to handle.

Case studies may be long (20 pages or more) or short (under half a page), but realism is always the key note. Problems may arise in choosing a situation to which all participants can relate. This is usually resolved by giving very detailed preliminary information, describing the situation and how it developed. Unfortunately, this can be so long and off-putting that participants at best just scan it. The amount of detail may be unavoidable. If so, pay particular attention to:

- Structure. Mention a topic in a single place only. Use headings to enable the student to refer back easily, even when developing the story line.
- Language. KISS, first and foremost. Then, consider that you are telling a tale. Novels often consist of at least one third dialogue to two thirds narrative. A case study may not be a novel, but conversation is an excellent way of 'lightening' the information and conveying emotion and personality. (Much more effective than writing: 'Mr Smith was angry'.)
- Layout. Use white space to make the writing attractive, and ensure that reference information (eg organization charts, timetables, financial projections etc) is easily found.
- Oral and visual presentation. It is also a good idea to present as much of the background information as possible orally and visually (tell the group the basic situation, display photographs of the main protagonists etc) before handing out the case study.

Since time spent understanding the background is largely wasted time (from a training point of view), it is worth only wasting it once. Have all case studies and role plays on a course relate to the same situation. This also adds to the continuity of the course, providing a link between the various sections.

Incidentally, you can buy books of non-copyright case studies. These can, however, be unnecessarily long and complex, and so, rather than using them as they are, adapt them to your purpose.

Remember, too, that short case studies can provide just as rich a learning experience as long ones. The alternative to lengthy background information is a situation which all participants can recognize at once. For example, here is a favourite case study of mine.

You are manager of a department. One of your subordinates has BO (body odour). You have noticed it yourself on several occasions, but said nothing hoping the problem would disappear. Now another subordinate has complained to you and asked you to do something about it. How would you handle the situation?

Figure 11.2 Short case study

Role plays

These may follow a case study discussion (for instance, the BO situation above), form part of a wider simulation (like a management game), or simply be introduced to enable students to practise communication skills.

They are often disliked by participants, who may feel nervous of exposing themselves, or consider the situation unreal and mere 'play-acting'. This unfortunately can get in the way of real learning, with participants reluctant to see any validity in the exercise. 'I wouldn't behave like that if I wasn't nervous / if it was a real situation' is a common disclaimer. There are several ways of combating this usually erroneous view.

Firstly, the trainer can, when introducing the exercise, point out that:

- Role plays are a concentrated experience, and most people therefore demonstrate a stronger, more concentrated version of their normal behaviour.
- It is the fact that role plays are a concentrated experience that makes them valuable, as concentrated behaviour is more obvious and therefore easier to analyse than 'real life' behaviour. It is not, however, fundamentally any different from 'real life' behaviour, just less dilute.
- Role plays are not intended as 'get-it-right' exercises, but are an opportunity to try out new forms of behaviour and learn from these. The debrief should be handled from this standpoint.

Secondly, the better the background briefing, the more comfortable most students feel with the exercise. This is a big advantage of linking role plays to a case study situation. Another way of increasing the realism of role plays is to base them on a real-life situation encountered by the participants.

Games

Games are also often referred to as 'simulations' or 'activities', although distinctions may be drawn between these. However, the term 'games' and in particular 'management games' is commonly used.

Games are long or short experiences, where the participants not only decide what to do about a situation (as in a case study, for instance), but also have to handle the results of their decisions.

Writing games is much more complicated than writing case studies. Many games and activities are available commercially, and I would suggest using a ready-made game rather than writing your own, provided, of course, that a ready-made one fits your requirements reasonably well. However, commercially-available games are written to cater for very general needs which may not match your particular situation. In that case, you may decide to devise your own.

Note the following points when writing text-based games:

- Depending on the skills being practised, the situation chosen may be less 'realistic' than for a case study. In the conventions of a management game, it is acceptable to choose situations which invite participants to suspend disbelief, such as crossing a desert or running a political election. However, the problem and solution must be internally consistent. If a 'realistic' situation is chosen (as is necessary for technical simulations and may be preferable for some management ones), it needs to be very realistic.
- Professional presentation of the materials (eg robust, laminated boards or cards) is critical. It encourages the participants to take the scenario seriously and thus aids the suspension of disbelief; it also lengthens the life of frequently-used materials.
- Test, test, test – not once but many times. Games are complex exercises and you are unlikely to be able to predict all reactions and outcomes. However, the more you try out the game, the more likely you are to discover what can go wrong and what to do about it.
- Include full trainer's notes and, if appropriate, a model solution. This should be presented in photocopiable form, as you are likely to want to hand it out to participants.

Mazes

These are also extensions of the case study, and may be considered as individual games. Typically, a situation is described, and a problem posed with a choice of three or four solutions. According to the solution chosen, the student is directed to different pages in the exercise. One solution is correct, or at least preferred; in the response, however, do explain why it is 'right' – the student may have picked it by chance or may not have been certain of the answer. Similarly, in the responses to the 'wrong' solutions, explain the reasons for not choosing them, and direct the student either back to the initial problem or on to the next stage of the exercise.

An alternative way of handling 'wrong' responses is to develop these situations too, creating different problems with exponentially-multiplying outcomes. Clearly there is a limit to the number of stages which you can introduce without burying the participant in paper. This approach is really only feasible with computer-based mazes, but even here the simple approach is generally the better one.

When using mazes take care to:

- Keep the situation at the right level of complexity as it develops through the various stages.
- Choose responses which are all realistic.

  'John finally emerges from his meeting and goes back to his desk. He looks at the mountain of paper in his in-tray. It is 6.30 pm and he is exhausted. Should he:
  a) make a start on it now?
  b) give up and go home?
  c) plan tomorrow's activities?'

- Respond to the 'right' solution with brief, non-patronizing, non-repetitive praise. Identify any disadvantages of the 'right' solution (as well, of course, as the advantages).

  'You thought John should give up and go home.
  You are right.
  John started his day early and he has not stopped rushing from one task to another. He badly needs to plan tomorrow's activities to avoid a repeat of today, but not now. Tomorrow morning he will feel fresher and will prioritize better.'

- Respond carefully to the 'wrong' solutions, so as not to discourage students. Identify any advantages of the 'wrong' solutions (as well as the disadvantages).

'You thought John should plan tomorrow's activities.
I don't agree.
You are right in saying that he badly needs to establish his priorities and
plan tomorrow's activities, but not now. He started his day early and has not
stopped rushing from one task to another. He is exhausted and in no fit
state to prioritize properly. Stress can be dangerous and John's most important
need at the moment is to go home and relax.'

- Make the link to the next problem a logical outcome of the solution.
- Offer a route map of 'right' answers for future reference.

In-basket exercises

These are also individual exercises. Students receive a package of documents
(letters, memos, copies of e-mails etc) which represent a typical in-basket and
which they have to handle, usually within a strict time limit. Although
commercial in-basket exercises exist, they are often less useful than trainer-written
ones which reflect the students' own in-baskets. When writing these exercises:

- Make sure that participants know what they are expected to do. For example,
  should they, in response to a particular document, just state that they would
  send an e-mail, or should they actually draft that e-mail?
- Include enough different documents to cause a variety of decisions to be
  made.
- Link some of the documents, so that a decision on one will have an impact
  on others.
- Ensure that the different documents reflect the different positions, per-
  spectives and personalities of their supposed authors.

Figure 11.3 shows an example of an in-basket introduction and Figure 11.4 of
a typical item.

Other exercises

Other written exercises can include tests and questionnaires (see Chapter 7).
With all such exercises, ensure that the questions cover the most important points,
by linking them directly with the exercise objectives.
There are a number of test formats:

- Multiple choice – *If. . ., would you a). . . b). . . or c). . . ?* Cynically called
  'multiple guess' because of the, often high, possibility of students choosing

In-basket exercise

You are John Baker, Office Services Manager.

A company organization chart and some additional information are attached to this exercise. The envelope clipped to the back of the exercise contains the contents of your in-basket.

It is Sunday 13 May, and you have just come back from three weeks' holiday. Dedication to duty (or a suspicion that there may be nasty surprises waiting for you) has prompted you to come into the office today to clear your in-basket. However, you do not want to spend more than half an hour on the task. A glance at your diary tells you that you have an appointment to see the Managing Director, Philip Smith, at 9.00 am on Monday morning. You have half an hour to go through your in-basket.

Note on each item how you would handle it. If you would speak to somebody about the item (either face-to-face or by phone), write down the gist of what you would say. If you would write to somebody about it, note briefly what you would write.

Figure 11.3 In-basket introduction

Memorandum

To: J Baker   Date: 27 April

From: P Smith

Subject: Security

It has come to my attention that unlawful entries have been made by strangers found on our premises.

This week, as I assume you have been informed, one miscreant was apprehended during the lunch hour, walking out with a personal computer.

That such an appalling situation could ever occur leads me to believe that we are extremely lax in our security arrangements.

I wish to discuss with you immediately you return from holiday what action you propose taking to tighten security arrangements.

Figure 11.4 In-basket item

the right answer by chance, these are nevertheless extremely useful exercises. They are flexible, quick to complete and simple to write and mark. Their validity increases if the 'wrong' answers (also known as 'distractors') are carefully chosen and phrased, as in the maze exercise examples above.

- Matching – *Which of the following items are connected?*
- Fill-in-the-blanks – *Insert the correct term in the following sentence.*
- True-or-false – *Which of the following statements are correct?*
- Sequencing – *Put the following items in order.*

(Like multiple choice questions, the last four types all mainly test discrimination and have limited validity. They too are quick and simple, but less flexible than multiple choice exercises.)

- Essay or free response – *Describe the relationship between. . .* Questions such as these are the only way of testing depth of knowledge and understanding, but they are hard to mark consistently. Model answers are a useful aid to consistent marking and also much appreciated by participants.

12

Self-learning Texts

Summary

Self-learning texts are very different from textbooks. With self-learning texts the emphasis is on helping the learner to learn. This chapter considers paper- and computer-based materials. Important aspects for both paper- and computer-based products are:

- having specific and detailed objectives;
- using graphics for visual relief and signposting;
- repeating information through summaries and checklists;
- using other media where appropriate;
- including exercises to give the learner practice;
- including tests to identify how well the objectives have been achieved;
- charting the complete self-learning package to show how sections interrelate;
- providing study advice;
- presenting the material in such a way as to encourage active participation;
- dry-running the material.

What are self-learning texts?

These are any written materials which are designed to help an individual learn on his or her own.

There have always been textbooks, of course, but many textbooks are passive in purpose – they aim simply to make information available. 'Helping an individual learn' means involving the learner actively, for instance by completing exercises, answering test questions, and applying the information to on-the-job situations.

There are many self-learning materials available commercially. You can even subscribe to databases which guide the trainer in choosing the most appropriate materials. Commonly called 'open learning' or 'distance learning' materials, they are the new generation of 'correspondence courses' or 'programmed instruction'.

Why should you write self-learning texts?

If there is so much available, you may think, why should you ever need to produce self-learning texts yourself? The obvious answer is: if there is nothing which meets your learners' exact needs.

One important example of this is induction, both to the company (new employees) and to a new job (promotions, transfers). A new job is a major stress event in a person's life. It is also a major opportunity for the employer. New job-holders often feel vulnerable and insecure. Make them feel 'part of the team' and they will stay on your side for ever. Induction training, which helps them to settle in quickly and get to grips with their new jobs, boosts morale *and* productivity – surely it is the magic answer to many management problems. And yet induction training, when it is given at all, is usually haphazard, half-hearted, and weeks (or months) too late. One of the main reasons for this is that new job-holders often are not 'they' (several at a time) but more likely 'he' or 'she'.

Self-learning materials are ideal for any training, like induction, which has to be:

- delivered promptly;
- repeated frequently;
- offered typically to few employees at any one time;
- capable of being offered in different locations, maybe at the same time.

Features of self-learning texts

Specific objectives

There are several important elements to remember when writing self-learning materials. Objectives, of course, are critical for all writing, but with self-learning texts they need to be developed to a finer level of detail.

For example, for a handout on, say, house layout style, you might have an overall objective that readers should know and be able to apply the house rules.

A self-learning text on the same topic would have several, more specific objectives.

'After completing this material you will be able to:

- Recognize our house layout style.
- Remember the different features of our house layout style.
- Identify which features of our house style are generally most important.
- Apply the house style to varied documents.
- In case of conflict, decide which features should be preferred, according to their relative importance and the document's purpose.'

Self-learning objectives should be spelt out clearly to the learners. This helps them map out where they are going and how much ground they have covered so far. Also, for some learners, for instance, recognizing the house style might be enough for their needs; they would therefore only complete the first part of the material.

Text

Text is the information-giving part of self learning materials. Again the principles are the same as for all writing. The normal question: 'How much information should you include?' is a key one; the answer is: 'Only as much as you need for the learner to achieve the objectives'. The more precise the objectives, the easier it is to write text.

In fact, actually writing the text may be best left until after you have written the tests (see below). This ensures a match between the tests and the information you have provided. On the other hand, writing in the order objectives–text–tests is more natural, and enables you to use the tests to double-check how appropriate and relevant both your objectives and text are.

Text should be written in easy-reading style – short and simple paragraphs, sentences and words. In particular, make sure that each paragraph only makes one point. A number of single-sentence paragraphs are much better, in self-learning materials, than one or two more literary, longer ones. And bullet points or, even more useful, numbering help the learner identify the separate points.

Language and tone should be conversational, direct and friendly. Address the reader as 'you'; avoid jargon; use contractions ('don't' etc) and colloquial phrases (eg 'have a go at'), although do be careful with anything too slangy. Such expressions date quickly and may offend some learners or be misunderstood by them, especially if English is not their first language.

Graphics

Also typical of self-learning materials is the use of graphics. Not just in illustration of points, although this is as important as with any other writing, but also graphic symbols, to indicate pictorially what the learner has to do next – an open book for 'read', a pen for 'write', a computer screen, video-tape, pair of headphones etc – as text is not the only way of giving information in self-learning packages. Also, cartoons and line drawings are used. These inject humour and lighten the learning. You can normally use graphics produced for other purposes, eg course visuals, in self learning texts, which can save you a lot of effort.

Summaries and checklists

These help the learner by providing:

- A quick reference to what is covered.
- Repetition. The common summary–text–checklist pattern matches the old training adage, 'First you tell them what you're going to tell them, then you tell them, then you tell them what you told them'.
- Pauses for reflection, because summaries and checklists are in a different format from the main text, and this encourages a change of pace in the reader.

Other media

As I mentioned, text is not the only way of giving information. Many commercial packages include computer presentations, video or audio materials. However, do not be seduced by this into thinking that *you* must include them in paper-based self-learning texts. Variation of media is certainly useful in maintaining the learner's interest, but only where the other media fulfil a purpose which text alone cannot achieve so well, such as showing actions or physical processes. If you can produce computer presentations, video and audio materials well and simply in-house, then they may be useful additions, but:

- The very high quality of leisure products in these fields has given learners exceptionally high expectations. Amateur production may destroy the credibility, and hence effectiveness, of materials, however well designed they are from a training point of view.
- Commissioning professional production is very expensive for video, and to a lesser extent, audio and computer materials.

- Copyright restrictions affect just about all commercially available products, so do not try your hand at editing without having first obtained permission.

This advice applies largely to paper-based products. I will discuss computer-based self-learning texts later in this chapter.

Exercises

As in face-to-face training, the aim is to provide the student with practice in demonstrating and applying the knowledge, understanding or skill that has been learnt. Many course exercises are perfectly suitable for self-learning.

Consider including case studies, individual games, mazes and in-baskets. Maze exercises are particularly useful; indeed these are fundamentally the same as 'programmed instruction', a long-established self-learning technique. There, an information block is followed by a multiple-choice question. 'Right' answers go on to the next information-block-plus-question; 'wrong' ones repeat the sequence or are directed to supplementary information.

Follow the basic approach outlined in Chapter 11, paying special attention to providing learners with feedback on their answers. As well as explaining what is 'right' or 'wrong', and why, you also need to offer the learner the 'personal' response which a course trainer would give. For example:

'I agree. I think this would work extremely well. . . .'
'This is a difficult problem. I would have tackled it this way.'
'Oops! Have you forgotten about. . . ?'

It is important to vary your comments. Repeating 'Well done!', 'Quite right!' or 'Sorry, think again about this one' 20 times sounds, and is, mechanistic, not personal.

Remember also to avoid sounding patronizing. This is difficult, especially as you are constantly trying to vary your wording. The best advice is to think of the learner as an intelligent friend. What would you *say* to him or her?

Tests

Tests are, of course, exercises too. The most common formats are:

- open questions and correct/model answers;
- multiple choice questions;

- matching;
- fill-in-the-blanks;
- true-or-false;
- sequencing.

The points made in Chapter 11 and above all apply when writing tests for self-learning materials.

All exercises test a learner's knowledge to a greater or lesser extent. However, with formal tests, the primary purpose is to identify to the learner how well the learning objectives have been achieved. Therefore you must ensure that your tests match your objectives and content.

One way of doing this is to write the tests as soon as you have prepared the objectives, and then write the text to match the tests. Another way, if you prefer to write the tests last, is to link particular test questions with particular objectives and information blocks. This way you can check if anything is missing, or has been given too much or too little emphasis.

Avoid one trap which is often tempting – writing test questions that only cover areas of knowledge that are easy to assess. Instead, make sure that your test questions cover the critical areas of knowledge.

Tests are normally carried out at the end of the programme or of a particular module or learning element. However, you can also use pre-programme tests to identify the learner's starting level of knowledge and vary the entry point to the programme appropriately.

Study aids

A distinguishing feature of self-learning materials is the 'help the learner to learn' approach. Deliberate attention is paid not just to the subject of the materials, but also to how the student can get the most out of them.

An especially useful aid is the flowchart or graphic representation of the complete self-learning package. This may show, for instance, which sections interrelate, key objectives for each session, and what activities the learner should perform. These may be an addition or an alternative to standard contents lists and indexes.

A second important study aid consists of advice on how to tackle the learning task. This may include hints on:

- scheduling priorities;
- selecting a convenient time and place for study;
- organizing the material;

- using reference documents, both external to the materials, eg a Thesaurus, and within the materials, eg an index or a glossary;
- reading attentively;
- writing answers;
- remembering information;
- applying it to the learner's job;
- preparing for exams.

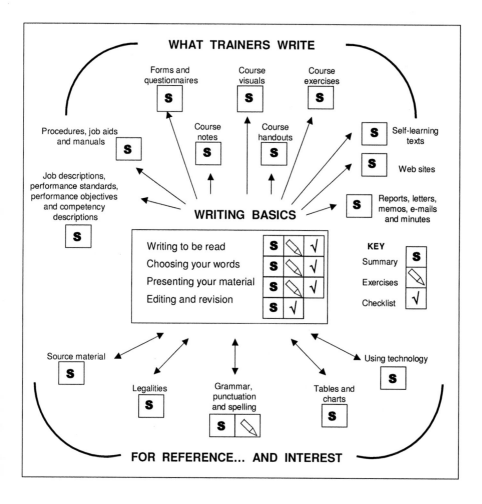

Figure 12.1 Study chart for this book

This advice may be concentrated at the beginning of the material, scattered throughout, or both.

What self-learning texts look like

In many ways the most distinguishing feature of self-learning materials is the appearance of the page. This is immensely important, and probably the greatest

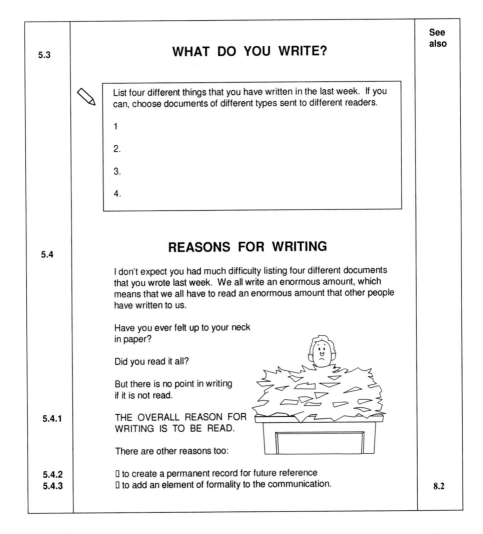

Figure 12.2 Self-learning text page

influence on whether people actually complete the self-learning text or merely skim through it.

Some characteristics of these pages are:

- Distinct layout – for example, white space, indentation, different length lines. Boxes around the exercises and different sized type highlight the change of activity. Different box designs can also be used to distinguish different types of activities.
- Making the structure obvious. The columns for section numbers and cross-references will be a standard throughout the self-learning text. Standard heading formats are used for each section.
- Graphics – charts, graphic symbols and cartoon drawings.

Incidentally, these pages have been produced using standard typing and photo-reduction, plus physical cut and paste. This is probably a sufficiently professional presentation for an in-house self-learning text, but proper printing or desk-top publishing (DTP) – see Chapter 19 – can make a great difference.

Computer-based self-learning materials

I deliberately did not call these self-learning texts as you should not try to transfer paper-based self-learning material onto a CD or a Web page and consider that a computer-based or e-learning product. Using the PC as an electronic page-turner is a waste of its potential and capacity, and the end-product would actually be much better as the workbook for which it was designed.

Writing Web-based self-learning products is really beyond the scope of this book, as they require not just writing techniques but an understanding of the technology of authoring computer systems. And e-learning is more than just the provision of Web-based products. (For more information, see Chapter 13).

Many excellent off-the-shelf computer- and Web-based products exist, although the majority concentrate on IT topics and knowledge transfer. However, as a trainer, you may need to design the content for your own specific exercises. Web-based products should be designed in a similar way to paper-based materials, in that they also should include:

- objectives;
- text;
- graphics;

- summaries and checklists;
- exercises;
- tests;
- study aids.

But Web-based learning products have very distinctive features and some enormous benefits:

- Web-based learning is a methodology which is becoming ever more attractive as we all become more IT-minded. 'Technophiles' love it! But people's expectations of both the technology and the content are extremely high, and professional presentation is paramount.
- The variety of content and media effects creates a much livelier product than a paper-based text, making it more likely that learners will stick with it. This is particularly true if there is human mentoring support for the learner.
- It allows for more, and more realistic, interaction between the learner and the material. For example, a case study or maze exercise can be turned into a role play, supported by technology and mentors to provide feedback and assistance to the learner.
- Multimedia effects, such as video and audio clips, provide more complete case studies and demonstrations.
- Exercises can be marked automatically, and the navigation path for maze exercises tailored to the learner's responses.
- Links to other material or references can be embedded in the text. Learners can simply click on these if they are interested in pursuing the topic further. If this linked material is updated at any time, the link can automatically take the learner to the updated version without needing to amend the Web-based learning product.
- Animation of graphics can be used to demonstrate processes.

Dry-running the material

Like all courses, self-learning materials, both paper- and computer- or Web-based, *must* be dry-run on potential users before being finalized. This can pose a timing problem for paper-based texts. Do you dry-run your material before or after it has been printed? Since the appearance of the material is so significant, it is less useful to dry-run before printing; on the other hand, reprinting because of changes can be very expensive, although fortunately this is becoming less of a problem with the wider use of DTP. Changes to Web-based material can also be complicated because of the design of the product and the inter-related links. Nevertheless, in all cases, these issues have to be accepted, as the products do have to be as high-quality as possible to catch and keep the learner's attention.

13

Web Sites

Summary

Training Web sites serve several purposes:

- marketing the training function;
- delivery of computer-based training (CBT) material and e-learning programmes;
- enabling automated course-booking and training record-keeping.

Although developing a Web site can require significant technical knowledge, there are now simple 'wizards' and templates which will enable non-IT specialists to set up a basic site. A Web site to market the training function is therefore within the province of most trainers. The development of sophisticated e-learning materials and automated booking and record-keeping systems are more complex and may require specialist assistance.

Why bother about a Web site?

The favourite cliché of annual reports – 'Our people are our greatest asset' – is no less true for being a cliché. Training is fundamental to the success of an organization, but it is often seen as a back-room, support function. 'Selling' the training function (in the sense of ensuring that business managers and employees can and want to make the best use of it) is a major part of every trainer's job. This is done by:

- forming close partnerships with business managers and employees to determine their needs;
- delivering events and resources to meet those needs in the most appropriate way;

- ensuring that the training function and its products are, *and are seen to be*, able to meet training needs competently and professionally.

Web sites are part of the new business image. Managers are accustomed to accessing them for information, so a training Web site is the ideal 'selling' tool. Use it to describe what you can offer managers and employees, and to make appropriate products available through the site, as easily and conveniently as possible.

What to include

The standard basic Web site format has four sections:

- About us;
- Products and services;
- More information;
- Contact us.

This format can easily be adapted to a training Web site. Let's look at each area. (You can, of course, change the section names.)

About us

This could include your functional goals, and how you hope to help managers and employees. It could feature names and photos of people in the department. (But do keep this current – there is nothing worse than out-of-date information.)

Products and services

Here you should probably include your catalogue of training courses, and also descriptions of other services you offer managers and employees, perhaps training needs analysis, individual coaching, career counselling, team building events, meeting facilitation, library facilities etc.

More information

This is where you can, if you wish, expand on your products and services (for instance, by including frequently-asked questions), and also make available any e-learning programmes that you wish to offer.

Contact us

Indicate here how people can take up your products and services. If you have a learning management system, employees or managers can check the availability of courses, make course bookings and receive joining instructions directly. They may also be able to access their individual training records. Even without such a system, however, include at the very least e-mail address links and telephone extensions (and do make sure they are kept up to date!).

Planning the site structure

Unlike a brochure where topics follow each other in a linear way, a Web site can accommodate all the complex interrelationships of a spider's web. Like the spider's web, it grows out of the centre, or home page, with links between the different elements.

As the very simplified Web chart in Figure 13.1 shows, it is important to plan the site structure first, to ensure that links are set up in the most efficient way. The mind map approach is useful for showing the linkages; you may also want to use an organization chart to plan the hierarchy of the pages. Do try to keep the hierarchy as shallow as possible – four levels, as in the example, is plenty.

The basic site structure is often made visible to users in the site header banner, in horizontal organization chart format. This helps users navigate around the site.

Drafting the content

Since there can be many routes to a particular page (such as the course catalogue page), you cannot assume that all site users will have reached it via any specific route. Therefore you need to ensure that each page stands on its own, and contains all the information necessary for it to be understood.

When writing text for a Web site, the points made in Part 1 of this book all apply. A few areas need to be emphasized or modified:

- Style. It is even more important than when using other media that your style is direct and even conversational – it is harder to read a computer screen than a paper document; therefore, take particular care to keep your language and content as short and simple as possible.
- Layout. Because of the restriction of displaying material on a small screen, layout should be uncluttered, and information produced in screen-sized bites.

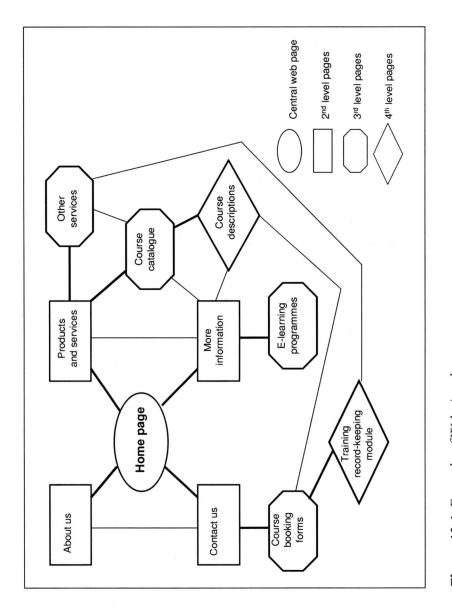

Figure 13.1 Example of Web site plan

Use the top left-hand corner of the screen for the most important items, as this is all that can be seen if the screen is reduced in size. Often this area is used for the site map. Header banners or sidebars are often used for illustrations or material which is interesting but not essential. Choose clear fonts and avoid the use of underlining for emphasis, as this may be confused with Web links.

- Pictures. Use visuals and animation, especially on the home page, but make sure that people can skip the multimedia effects if they wish, as they may require additional 'plug-in' packages or take a long time to download.

'Wizards' and templates

These will guide the novice through the process of setting up a basic Web site. They will allow you to:

- set up pages;
- insert links between them;
- choose your colour scheme and letter fonts;
- add text and visuals;
- insert links to other sites.

You may well, however, have a company house style for Web sites, so do consult your IT department if appropriate.

It is essential to test out your Web pages, to ensure that they really do look and work as you intended.

E-learning programmes

Web sites are an excellent way of delivering electronic self-learning materials, as described in Chapter 12. E-learning programmes, however, comprise more than these materials. They are complete training courses, delivered wholly or largely by electronic means. They typically feature:

- Electronic self-learning materials.
- Access to other electronically-held information, for instance company presentations and video materials.
- Access to the tutor via e-mail – the more frequent and personalized this is, the more effective the learning is likely to be.
- Access to other students through chat rooms, set up as pages where students may ask questions and exchange information and views. Much of the benefit

from any training course comes from talking to other students, and this should therefore be encouraged. One way of doing this, if a number of students will be completing an e-learning programme at about the same time, is to incorporate a face-to-face or video-conference 'getting to know each other' session for all participants.

The benefit of e-learning programmes is that participants can learn at their own pace, in their own time (although, as we have seen, synchronization does allow better contact between learners), and in their own way. When designing e-learning programmes, it is important for both the trainer and the learner to be aware of the learner's preferred learning style, and to accommodate this as far as possible.

Course-booking and record-keeping systems

Electronic course booking systems usually consist of:

- Access to course availability information, so that students can check which courses have vacant places.
- Web booking forms, normally completed by the employee. The general design of these should follow the principles in Chapter 7. Specialized computer packages exist to help you set up these forms or, if you don't have access to such a package, consult your IT department.
- Automated approval systems. After the employee completes the booking form, the system will send a standard e-mail to the employee's manager requesting confirmation of the booking, and usually a cost code to link into an internal finance system.
- Automatic booking of participants, and confirmation of joining instructions to the employee and manager.

These systems are often part of more extensive training record-keeping or learning management systems. These are complex to set up, and normally require specialist IT assistance.

Such systems often allow employees and their managers access to the employee's training records. Do ensure that you comply with data protection legislation.

Maintaining your site

Although I have mentioned several times already that it is critical to ensure that your site is regularly maintained, this is worth emphasizing. Check frequently that links still work; and that names, e-mail addresses, telephone numbers and organizational descriptions are current.

If you make any part of your site unavailable to users (for instance, while you are updating it), ensure that you tell users who try to access that part what you are doing.

14

Reports, Letters, Memos, E-mails and Minutes

Summary

For completeness, this chapter looks at the standard writing tasks that trainers also need to perform – reports, letters, memos, e-mails and minutes of meetings. As these are discussed in many other books, I will not cover them in any detail. Word processing packages contain standard templates for all these writing tasks, but you may prefer to use your own approach to suit your reader's needs.

- Reports are most effective when written with the reader clearly in mind. SOPORRA (Summary – Objective – Position – Options – Recommendation – Required action – Appendices) is a useful structure.
- Letters need to combine effectiveness with a polite, personal approach. The structure PRRR (Position – Response – Request – Respects) helps to achieve this.
- Memos may be mini-reports or internal letters. Consider first whether they need to be sent at all.
- E-mails are electronic letters or memos. Only write necessary e-mails, and only copy those people who need to receive them. Check the wording before sending e-mails.
- Minutes should be written in a format which identifies actions to be implemented. They may be written during the meeting itself.

Reports

Reports are rarely popular. They are often too long (which makes them a chore both to write and read); they are written in a formal, indirect style (which is meant to impress, but doesn't); and they frequently fail to achieve their objectives.

Unfortunately, trainers may not be able to avoid writing reports. The UK National Standards for Training and Development refer to many different proposals that trainers should make, for instance proposals which identify:

- the strategic contribution of training;
- human resource needs to carry out the strategy;
- training needs for those human resources;
- training resource needs to carry out the training.

And that is only in section A1! How do you submit all these proposals? Usually, as reports.

The main problem with reports is that they are often written to boards and committees – in other words to a number of people, some (even many) of whom the writer may not know. In trying to play safe and cover all contingencies, the report only serves as a graveyard for the good ideas buried inside. The points made in Chapter 1, about getting to know your readers and identifying their needs, are critical. If different readers may have conflicting needs, focus on those of the most influential reader (who is not always the most senior one):

- What does he or she already know about the subject? (Don't repeat it.)
- What are likely to be his or her concerns? (Treat them seriously.)
- What are likely to be his or her priorities? (Reflect them in your arguments.)
- Address his or her likely prejudices. (Either pander to them, or refute them with unemotional, non-critical logic.)

It is easier to keep reports short and to the point if you follow a set structure. I hate to suggest SOPORRA as a mnemonic as the last thing you want your reports to be is soporific! However, let's examine this structure.

As already mentioned, SOPORRA stands for:
Summary – Objective – Position – Options – Recommendations – Required action –Appendices.

A *summary* is only needed for reports of 4–5 pages or more. It should be no more than 10 per cent of the length of the whole report, ie summarize 4–5 pages in half a page maximum, 9–10 pages in one page maximum. (And try to keep the report to 10 pages at most.) Although it is often easiest to write the summary after the bulk of the report, it is very helpful for busy readers to find it on the front page, where they can scan it quickly as soon as the report is picked up. Carefully-bound reports, with title and contents sheets and the summary buried on page 2 or 3, look attractive, but are less in tune with the reader's needs, and often get pushed to the bottom of the pile 'until there is time to read them'.

The **objective** (scope, terms of reference etc) should be stated briefly to ensure that your readers do not have the wrong expectations. For example, 'In this report, I recommend measures for training supervisors. I will consider management training separately in a later report'.

Next outline the current **position**. This may include some background information, but only if it is required to enable your readers to understand your recommendations, and only if they do not already know it.

If it is important to show that you have not skimped your research, mention briefly the various **options** you considered and discarded, and then home in on your chosen **recommendations**, giving your conclusions, the reasons for your choice, likely outcomes, timescales and costs.

Many reports reach this point, but then founder and achieve nothing. This may be because the report itself has not specified what **required action** should now be taken, by whom and by when. Spelling this out will make it more likely that your recommendations will be implemented or, if they are rejected, may give you an opportunity to revise and resubmit your proposals.

Appendices should contain all the information which the reader needs to know but which is too detailed to be included in the body of the report. Wherever possible, present calculations and statistical charts and tables as an appendix. Do not feel, however, that you must have appendices, and put in masses of merely 'nice to know' information, just to impress your readers. It will, on the contrary, only irritate them.

The different sections of a report should be identified with separate headings and subheadings. This makes the argument clearer for the reader and allows easy reference to other sections. It is similarly often helpful to number sections and subsections.

Letters

Business letters should be polite, personal and effective. They should achieve your objective and enhance your relationship with your reader.

The first difficulty often comes right at the beginning. What do you call your reader? 'Dear Mike' or 'Dear Mary' is suitable if you know the person well enough, and if the informality is appropriate to the tone and content of your letter. 'Dear Mr Smith' may seem safe in response to a letter signed 'M Smith', but it will hardly enhance your relationship with Mary Smith, let alone Dr Smith or Professor Smith. Getting someone's name wrong is a fundamental insult. It is worth a few minutes' research (check previous correspondence, ask colleagues, even telephone M Smith's secretary) to avoid this sort of mistake.

If you do not know whether the woman to whom you are writing is married, you have the choice of:

- 'Dear Miss Smith' (This used to be conventional; it is much less acceptable these days.)
- 'Dear Ms Smith' (Many people hate it, but it is convenient.)
- 'Dear Mary Smith' (Personally, I always think this reads oddly, but it is an alternative to 'Ms' which is gaining in popularity.)
- 'Dear Madam' (This sounds stilted and formal.)

If you do not know your reader's name, 'Dear Sir' or 'Dear Madam' is conventional. 'Dear Sir or Madam' sounds like the opening of a government circular.

The beginnings of letters are prone to 'commercialese'. 'With regard to your esteemed favour of 14th inst' may be moribund, but it is all too often replaced with 'Re your letter dated. . .'

'Thank you for your letter of. . .' is polite and avoids a sentence structure which can otherwise sometimes be tortuous.

It is a good idea to start a letter with a heading giving the subject of the letter – this concentrates the reader's mind and aids efficient filing. Incidentally, there is no reason why longer business letters, covering several points, should not include subheadings or section numbers. As in reports, these add clarity to the structure.

A mnemonic for structuring letters is PRRR. (Purr-fect letters?)
Position – Response –Request –Respects

In the **position**, outline or refer to what has happened so far, but do not dwell on anything your reader already knows. The **response** is what is actually causing you to write the letter.

The **request** or recommendation should be expressed from the reader's point of view. Writing 'you' as much as possible will make your arguments more persuasive: 'You will benefit from this by. . .' rather than: 'I recommend this because. . .'. Make the request or recommendation precise by specifying the required action (who needs to do what, how, where, and when).

And end by paying your **respects**. Politeness is important, but it is sometimes difficult to steer between the weak or meaningless: 'I look forward to hearing from you', and the sometimes abrupt or aggressive: 'Unless I hear from you by next Monday, I shall. . .'

Write your ending to suit your reader, but in general the more polite, positive and specific your choice of words, the more likely you are to achieve your objective.

The final salutation should match the initial form of address: 'Dear (name). . . Yours sincerely'. 'Dear Sir. . . Yours faithfully'.

And to save your reader problems when replying to your letter, include with your name any particular form of address you prefer (eg Miss, Mrs, Ms, Dr etc).

Memos

Memos are usually written in response to memos received; they themselves often generate further memos in reply, which in turn. . .

Think very carefully before writing a memo. Is it necessary? Would a telephone call serve your purpose better? Can you reply in a few words handwritten on the original?

Memos may be mini-reports, or letters sent to colleagues within your organization. Follow whichever guidelines seem appropriate, and your house style regarding salutation and signature. This may range from omitting both (the sender's and receiver's names merely being typed at the top of the memo), to inserting a handwritten 'Dear John' at the beginning of the memo and 'Cordially, Bill' at the end. This second approach is more typical of US than British organizations.

E-mails

E-mails are rapidly taking over from internal memos, and even from letters to people outside your organization. In some ways, they are also replacements for meetings and conversations. However, they are a written and not a spoken form of communication, and do need to be treated as such. Generally, consider them either as letters or memos, and use the appropriate structure, language and forms of salutation.

E-mails do have two obvious but critical features which distinguish them from letters or memos – ease and speed.

Firstly, they are seductively easy to compose and, because they seem such an informal medium, it may seem as if any style or language is appropriate. And it is tempting to send e-mails constantly and to everybody who may be (however remotely) concerned with your message. Net result, in some companies people may receive well over a hundred e-mails a day and, from sheer self-preservation, people delete many of them unread!

Secondly, you can dispatch your e-mail immediately you have drafted it, so writers may not check and reflect on the content before pressing the send button.

These two features can create pitfalls for the unwary e-mail writer:

- Identifying your reader and writing for him or her is at least as critical with e-mails as with other forms of writing. Remember that, as with all writing, you need to write what your reader needs to read, not just what you want to say. Competition for your reader's reading time is more acute than ever, with all those other e-mails clogging up his or her in-box. A reputation as somebody who only sends necessary and appropriate e-mails will ensure that yours are given reading priority above those of other people, and will keep your reader's finger off that delete button.
- When replying to an e-mail, do not automatically copy everybody who received the original mail – if they do not need the information, they will certainly be grateful and not offended at being excluded from your reply!
- You need to attract your reader's attention from the very beginning – in the subject line. Make sure that this is specific and tells your reader what the e-mail is about. E-mails with subjects like 'Various' or 'Miscellaneous' deserve to be deleted unread. It is better to send several e-mails, one covering each separate item (provided that each item is really worthy of being the subject of an e-mail) than batching topics in the same message under a general heading. This also helps the reader's filing of the e-mails.
- You can make your e-mail stand out in your reader's inbox by using colour for your header details. Alternatively, you can give the message a high priority, or make the first word of the subject 'Urgent' or 'Important'. Don't do this unless it is true!
- When attaching documents and other files to your message, be careful of anything with graphics and animation – they take a lot of space and may slow down the system.
- If you have a company house style, or a formal disclaimer that must be used on all external correspondence, do ensure that you comply with these requirements. E-mails are as legally binding as any other correspondence.
- Think before using capitalization. Beware of using capitals to give emphasis to words or phrases in your message – in e-mail etiquette, they come across as aggressive 'shouting'. Equally, do not be so lazy and casual as to send everything in lower case – use initial capital letters in exactly the same way as you would in any other written document.
- Proofread and spellcheck your e-mails before sending them, and make sure that you actually have attached any files that you wish to send with the message. A follow-up e-mail saying 'Sorry, here is the attachment' is not a good advertisement of your professionalism. (Incidentally, sending is not always irrevocable – just in case, do mke sure you know, how to retrieve unread e-mails!)

- Be careful about sending hasty e-mails and responses, especially if you are annoyed or feel strongly about something. Reflect first on how your e-mail will be received. Although you can send e-mails at almost the speed of speech, they are a permanent record of your words and can appear more inflammatory because of that. Indeed, e-mail jargon has coined the term 'flame mail' to describe angry or provocative messages which are later regretted by all concerned.
- Finally, a word about signatures. It is useful to include telephone contact details in your sign-off, if only to avoid a lengthy e-mail correspondence which would have been better dealt with by a quick telephone call. However, don't make your signature too long, as it just takes up space!

Minutes

Minutes are a formal record of all points discussed or decided in a meeting. That does not imply that they can or should be a verbatim transcript of all that was said. They are a factual summary, and one of their most important practical functions is to ensure that all actions agreed by the meeting are implemented. A simple format can help this to happen.

Those present:		Date:	
Agenda item	Discussion/Action	Who?	When?

Figure 14.1 Format for meeting minutes

Such brief minutes can actually be written during the meeting, copied and handed to the participants at the end. This obviously encourages action to be taken promptly, but it has another advantage. By summarizing each major discussion point briefly to the meeting and then recording it, the minute-writer both contributes to the efficient conduct of the meeting, and ensures that the minutes are correct and agreed at the time.

Standard templates

Word processing packages contain standard templates and 'wizards' to guide you through all these writing tasks. However, you may prefer to use your company house style if there is one, or just your own layout to reflect your reader's needs and priorities.

Part 3
For Reference...
and Interest

15

Source Material

Summary

The two main sources of training material are people and documents.

'People' sources include company colleagues, training course participants, professional colleagues outside your company and librarians or information assistants. Confidentiality must be observed when using real experiences for training material.

Information from people is usually written down at some stage and becomes a 'paper' source. Other 'paper' sources include books, magazines, company documents, training materials already written (by yourself or others), publicity material about external courses and products etc. In this chapter I use the US Armed Service Technical Information Agency documentation system as an example: it allows quick and easy filing and retrieval of this mass of information.

Written information can also be found on the Internet, which is an invaluable and extremely convenient information source. However, searches need to be tightly targeted, otherwise you can spend a lot of time looking at irrelevant documents. Accuracy of the information may also need to be checked.

Sources

Every trainer needs to use other sources in order to get ideas and information for training materials. This can be a rather haphazard process:

'Now, wasn't I speaking to someone about that recently? Was it at the training association branch meeting, or at that film launch, or at the exhibition last month. . . ? And who was it, anyway?'
'I'm sure I read an article about that. Where can it be?'
'There has to be masses of stuff about this on the Web, but how do I find it?'

Sources generally come in two shapes – people and paper (including the 'electronic paper' of the Internet). This chapter will cover methods of searching for information and of organizing your source materials for easy retrieval.

People

All writers use other people as sources for what they write, and trainers are no different in this from any group of writers. 'People' sources for trainers include colleagues (both inside and outside the organization), trainees and official information-givers (librarians etc).

Most trainers try to pick the brains of managers in their company to get information for teaching points, exercises, case studies etc. This is intended to give their material the 'real-life' validity which trainees seek, and which helps convince management of the relevance of the training. Unfortunately, much of this 'company background' is (and appears to be) a superficial gloss rather than fundamental to the material. This is often because the use of this company information is unplanned and comes too late in the course design process. As well as pre- and post-course discussions with participants' managers, the best time to collect this sort of information is when initially discussing training needs – all those grumbles about what people can't do should not only govern the training objectives, but can also provide many specific examples to use within the material. Remembering these examples, of course, can be a problem, so don't try – write them down and file them as suggested below, and then you will have them easily accessible to use from the earliest stage of the course design.

An important point to consider is confidentiality, but usually false names and discreet changes of department or background are enough to protect the protagonists. However, do not be surprised if your trainees know more than you do about the situation, or think they do. I once used a case study about a manager with a 'drink problem'. I camouflaged his identity very successfully, only to have the trainees identify the character as somebody else!

Training course participants themselves are obviously another excellent source of material. Asking them, before the course, to choose and be prepared to discuss four or five relevant situations which they have experienced makes their contributions richer and more varied. Confidentiality is again paramount, both from yourself and from the other course members. It may be that some of these experiences provide such powerful learning material that you would like to use them on other courses – this must only be with the individual's permission and with any identifying details altered.

Confidentiality is less of a problem with situations related by colleagues outside your company, provided, once more, that identities are concealed. In order to milk this rich information source fully, a little organization and a card case are required. Exchange business cards with external colleagues, and do not just thrust the card in your pocket and forget about it. When turning out your pockets that evening, note on the back of the card when and where you met the person and the main topics you talked about, and then keep the card in your card case. The frustration saved is more than worth the effort.

And don't forget the 'official' sources of material. Information services, professional or management organizations, libraries are all there to help you, so use them. Appendix 3 lists a number of organizations I use, but you may want to compile your own list (add contact names wherever you can) and keep it handy for reference.

Paper

In order to avoid having to remember, and forgetting, all the information you glean from these 'people' sources, you need to write it down and be able to find it again when you want it.

The same is true of all your other 'paper' sources of material:

- books and magazines;
- company documents (procedures, forms, reports etc);
- training courses (lesson plans, handouts etc), your own and those other people have given you, current courses and old ones;
- publicity information (covering external courses, training films, generic training materials etc).

Over a number of years this adds up to a huge pile of paper. You need a filing system that enables you to: identify instantly whether you have any information on a given subject; retrieve, in minutes, all the information you have on that subject – even find an article you read five years ago and had forgotten about, but which is just what you need now.

The simplicity of the US Armed Service Technical Information Agency Uniterm System for Coordinate Indexing belies the complexity of its name. Once the system has been set up, filing documents is straightforward and retrieving them unbelievably easy. (If I sound enthusiastic, I am.)

To start the system, take any document you want to keep. Give it a number – start with 1 and continue in strict numerical order – and write the number actually on the document. Then consider what the document is about. Jot down all the keywords that describe for you what that document covers, again either on the front of the document or on a piece of paper stapled to it, if that is more convenient. For instance, a handout for a writing skills course might have 'Training', 'Handout' and 'Writing' as keywords. These are the classifications by which the document will be filed and retrieved.

These keywords, and those for all the other documents you wish to keep, are the basis of the filing system. You may think that you would have an infinite number of keywords, but in fact the same ones will crop up repeatedly, reflecting your interests and concerns. In a fully developed system about 500–1000 keywords are normally used. The filing system may be organized manually with index cards, or electronically on a spreadsheet. You have one card or line per keyword, and on it you list all the document numbers of documents with this keyword. (If you are keeping a manual record, you also need alphabetical index cards, listing all your keywords for that letter.) And that is the whole system.

To file a document, write its number and keywords on the document itself and record its number on all the appropriate keyword cards or lines. If you need to create a new keyword card, do so, simply adding it to the alphabetical list. Physically file the documents themselves in numerical order.

To retrieve a document, consult the alphabetical list to see if you have filed any documents for the keywords you want. It does help to avoid synonyms – for instance, do not have both 'Aim' and 'Objective' as keywords, but choose one and stick to it. If the word is listed, the keyword card will give you the numbers of all the documents on that topic. Now you may not want *all* the documents associated with a particular keyword, so you can combine the keyword cards to narrow your choice.

When you are hunting for a Writing Skills course handout, 'Training' might produce a list of, say, 200 documents, but only 20 of those numbers appear also on the 'Writing' card and only 2 of these on the 'Handout' card – a manageable number.

Date keywords (eg '2001') are useful if you want to weed your filing system periodically. You probably will not want to do that with all documents but some, such as publicity material, may only have a short-term relevance. In that situation, include the date when you want to review or discard the material as an additional keyword. At the end of the period, you can retrieve all dated material and decide whether or not to keep it. If you want to discard it, throw it away and cross the document number off all the associated keyword cards. (You know what they are because they are written on the front of the document.)

This system takes a little time to set up, but once in use it is simple and foolproof.

Information on the Internet

The amount of information available on the Internet is such that you may feel that any other research method has become redundant. You can find Web sites, documents, images, sound and video clips, all without moving from your desk. But reaching relevant information is not always as easy as you might think, simply because of the vast amount available.

Search engines function on a keyword basis. They will scan Web sites for documents (or pictures etc) which match your selected keywords and phrases. This is a similar approach to the manual information retrieval system which I described above; the difference lies in the number of documents stored in the system. When you run a search, you may find that there are 20,000 or more documents which contain your keywords – clearly a daunting situation! Irrelevant data is the biggest problem for Web research. The more specific your keywords, the more likely you are to find relevant documents.

In fact, even those 20,000 documents will not include every possible match which is on the Internet. Different search engines cover different sites, so it is worth using more than one engine if you are having difficulty finding relevant information.

Another issue concerns the accuracy and reliability of the information. Unlike published books, magazine articles or academic papers, Web sites do not have to be reviewed by anybody except the writer, and out-of-date material is as easily accessible as current information. Do check any information which is not current and not from an authoritative source.

All this may sound as if using the Web is more effort than it is worth. Certainly there does need to be some effort, but the potential coverage and convenience are so great that, to my mind, they far outweigh the difficulties. A few guidelines may help:

- Make your keyword selection as precise as possible. The search engines' 'hint' or 'tip' pages can help here. If your keyword has a number of possible meanings, specify also terms which you do *not* want to see. For instance, when searching for information about the World Wide Web, it may be useful to specify that you do not want to see any documents containing the word 'spider'.
- Use several search engines, as they may come up with different documents in the early matches. (In principle, these should be the most relevant, given your keyword combination, but don't count on it!) You can also use 'meta' search engines which scan a number of engines at once.
- Check the accuracy of the information if you possibly can, especially if it was published some time previously.

- Remember that documents on the Web are subject to copyright – downloading a file, saving or printing it are all forms of 'copying'. To be able easily to gain access to sites or documents later, without breaching copyright, you need to set up a spreadsheet index in much the same way as recommended for the manual system. The only difference is that, instead of physical pieces of paper, you store Web addresses and the appropriate keywords.
- Use Web-based newsgroups, chat rooms and discussion forums to seek help, information and advice from other people, but, once more, remember that it may be wise to check the accuracy of this information.

16

Legalities

Summary

There are two main aspects of law which impact trainers – copyright and data protection.

When using outside source materials you may well have to consider the question of copyright. This chapter looks at:

- what copyright is;
- what works are subject to copyright;
- how long copyright lasts;
- what constitutes breaches of copyright, and exceptions to the rules.

If you want to use a work that is protected by copyright for training purposes in your organization, you either need to seek permission from the copyright owner, or reword and develop the ideas for yourself, relating them to your own organization.

When keeping training records, especially on a company Web site, you also need to consider data protection legislation. This requires you to protect personal information about individuals, ensuring that it is not available to people who do not have a business need to see it. Also, unless the individual has given consent, the information may not be transmitted across national boundaries to countries where there is less rigorous legislation, for instance the United States.

Disclaimer

I want to start this chapter with a disclaimer. I am not a lawyer, and I am not competent to and do not pretend to give legal advice. In this chapter, I am simply setting out the broad principles behind UK copyright and data protection law, and indicating in very general terms whether a work is likely to be subject to copyright, and what data protection constraints you should consider.

However, legislation is extremely complex. *If you have any specific concerns, check with a lawyer who specializes in this area.* Lawyers' fees are cheaper than damages!

What is copyright?

Copyright is a right, which entitles the owner of an original, created work to prevent other people from copying or publishing that work, or a substantial part of it, for a certain period of time.

'Work' covers, among others, literary, artistic, dramatic and musical works. It includes sound recordings, films and computer programs. The most important works from the point of view of the trainer are:

- Written works. 'Literary', the term used in the legislation, is a catch–all phrase which does not imply artistic merit. Memos and letters are 'literary' works; so are tables of numbers and computer programs; so, of course, are published books and articles. Web sites and the information stored on them are covered in exactly the same way as paper documents.
- Charts, plans, sketches, photographs etc. These are also subject to copyright, but they are classed as 'artistic' works.
- Videos and films.
- Audio cassettes.

'Copying' means, very roughly, any form of reproduction, whether or not the copy is shown to other people. The reproduction has to be of the *form* of the work – the actual words which were written, the pictures, the film etc, and *not just* the ideas which those words, pictures or film express. Downloading and saving or printing a computer file is considered copying. 'Publishing' means distributing, performing or making available to other people.

The restricted period of time is, most commonly: for written work, 70 years after the death of the creator of the work; for videos etc, 70 years after the death of the director, author or composer, whichever is last.

These are gross simplifications. Copyright law is a minefield, with a number of successive Acts each adding its quota of amendments, additions and exceptions. As I said, if in doubt, consult a lawyer.

What works are protected by copyright?

There are two principal factors to consider: time and place.

The consideration of **time** is that, generally, written works are protected until 70 years after the year when their author died.

When considering **place**, bear in mind that UK copyright law covers works by British citizens and works published in the UK and certain other countries. However, international copyright conventions, which the UK has signed along with most other countries, mean that we offer the same protection to works of foreign nationals as we do to those written by British citizens. (Similarly, UK copyright owners are protected overseas, although each country may have particular requirements, for example US copyright must be registered and, in the past, regularly reviewed.)

In general, assume that most material you will want to use is protected.

What can you not do?

You are not allowed to carry out 'restricted acts'. These are, of course, only restricted if they apply to a work protected by copyright. As far as the trainer is concerned, the main restricted acts are:

- Copying a work or a substantial part of one. This includes copying by hand, typing, photocopying, photographing, faxing, computer scanning, saving or printing a computer file, filming, sound recording, video copying, audio cassette or CD copying – in fact, assume it covers *any* form of copying. Exact copying, for instance taking photocopies, photographs, computer scans or facsimile copies, may in addition infringe the copyright of the typographical layout owned by the publisher of the work.
- Issuing copies of the work, or playing or performing it in public.
- Adapting a work. This covers translations, and converting a work from one medium to another, for example transcribing the words of a video and using this as a case study, or transferring text-based materials onto a computer.
- Importing, possessing, distributing or showing any copy of a work, which you have reason to believe was made in breach of copyright.
- Many Web sites have copyright agreements, which you have to accept before being able to enter the site. These agreements specify in detail what may and may not be done.

Exceptions

There are some situations in which a 'restricted act' may not infringe copyright. The important ones which affect trainers are:

- Copying, quoting or publishing less than a 'substantial' part of the work. Unfortunately, there is no fixed definition of 'substantial' and importance counts at least as much as length. It may be considered that anything important enough to copy is important enough to protect.
- Copying, quoting or publishing for purposes of research and private study. If you are preparing a training course and need to research a particular aspect, you are entitled to make copies of works to help you in that research. However, that only applies to *your* research and private study; you may not share your copies with colleagues or students.
- Copying for purposes of criticism and review. If you are criticizing or reviewing a work, you may reproduce parts of that work in your review, provided that you give 'sufficient acknowledgment' ie identify the work by author and title.
- Copying, quoting or publishing for reading and recitation. These are permitted, provided that you make sufficient acknowledgment.
- Copying, quoting or publishing materials for use in educational establishments. Educational establishments are defined in the legislation as schools and institutions for Higher and Further Education. Representatives of these establishments may copy material except printed music for examinations and, subject to restrictions, for instruction. Blanket licences also exist, like the one issued by the Copyright Licensing Agency which covers all local authority schools. If you do not know whether your organization qualifies as an educational establishment, or is covered by a licence, contact the National Council for Educational Technology (see Appendix 3 for the address).

Permission to copy or publish

If you want to carry out a restricted act in respect of a work that is subject to copyright, you need to get permission from the copyright owner. This is initially the author or employer (if the work was produced by an employee during the course of employment). The Crown is the first owner of copyright of any work produced by an officer or servant of the Crown (including all government and civil service employees) during the course of his or her duties.

The ownership of copyright may be assigned permanently to another person or a temporary licence may be given. In seeking permission to copy or publish material, contact the current owner (author, employer or assignee) or any licence holder.

The publisher of the work can usually put you in contact with the author, and may even handle your request on the author's behalf. If you want to reproduce not only the content but also the typographical arrangement of the work, you need the publisher's permission as well as that of the author.

When seeking permission, be specific as to *exactly* what material you want to copy or publish, and what you intend to do with it. Always offer full acknowledgment of the author and the work. You are likely to have to pay a fee. The amount will vary according to the material and the use you want to make of it.

Data protection

Individuals have the right to know what information is held about them, unless that would breach somebody else's data protection rights. Individuals are also entitled to have personal data kept and processed, in such a way that:

- The data is only used for the purpose for which it was collected. For instance, if you say that course test performance is solely for use within the course, the ratings cannot be used in performance appraisals or disciplinary proceedings for poor performance.
- The data that is kept is relevant and not excessive for the stated purpose. It must be accurate and kept up to date, and not kept for longer than necessary. Do you, for instance, need to keep detailed training records after somebody has left the company?
- Data is only made available to those people who need to see it in order to carry out the stated purpose. It may well be appropriate to share performance data from a recent training course with the individual's manager, but perhaps not past courses.
- Data is not transferred outside Europe (EEA), except to countries with equivalent data protection rights. Currently, this would exclude the United States. This can be a problem if your company uses global databases, which are physically kept outside Europe. Many companies who are headquartered or have a significant presence in the United States ask their employees to sign data consent forms, agreeing to the transmission of their data outside Europe.

If your course booking and training records are Web-based, you may well wish to have an introductory screen explaining the purpose and the use which will be made of any data. This might also include a specific acceptance of that use by the individual. However, if all employees have signed broad data consent forms in any case, this may not be necessary. Yet again, it is advisable to consult a lawyer.

17

Grammar, Punctuation and Spelling

Summary

Grammar, punctuation and spelling are the nuts and bolts of writing. Their purpose is to enable you to communicate your meaning, and their rules are intended to clarify, not mystify. People are often wary about grammar, punctuation and spelling, usually as a result of half-forgotten schoolday maxims and terrifying schoolteachers. But this is unnecessary – grammar, punctuation and spelling are not difficult and, used well, will ensure that your reader understands your message as you intend it. Used badly, they will irritate and confuse.

This chapter is not an exhaustive description of all the linguistic rules and exceptions. It will, however, give you an overview of the main points, and will look at some of the more common trouble spots.

'Grammar is bunk' – but is it?

Many people, remembering their schooldays, might be tempted to misquote Henry Ford, and maintain that 'Grammar is bunk' and boring bunk at that. It is not. But equally it is not the holy shrine that pedants would make it. Schoolteachers preaching inflexible commandments, couched in incomprehensible jargon, have a lot to answer for. Grammar is a template, a pattern to help you make your meaning clear to your readers, not iron bonds to constrain you.

Yes, there are rules, and they are worth following in almost all instances – after all they have a long and honourable pedigree. If English is your mother tongue, you almost certainly do follow them naturally most of the time. But language develops and usage seems to have outstripped some of the rules. Feel free to ignore a rule if you think it will confuse rather than clarify your meaning, *provided that you are sure your reader will not misjudge you and think you ignorant.*

Many people have fixations about grammar, based on those childhood precepts dinned in with a sledgehammer:

- Never split an infinitive.
- Never start a sentence with 'and' or 'but'.
- Never end a sentence with a preposition.

I admit to being rather an un-split infinitive person myself, but even I can understand why you might want to boldly sunder the two parts. The meaning is clear – clearer than 'boldly to sunder. . .' or 'to sunder. . . boldly'. And, as you can see, the other two maxims I have even fewer qualms about.

Let's examine this grammatical template in more detail. The verbal strip cartoon shown in Figure 17.1 introduces many of the main parts of speech and grammatical constructions. Refer back to it, if you are unsure of any of the terms mentioned later in this chapter.

Grammar – points to consider

Verbs

Some areas of grammar are more prone to cause confusion than others. Verbs are common sinners. Here are a few points to consider.

Passives can lead to problems (as I have discussed in earlier chapters): *The trainer was told that. . .* is not specific and can therefore lead to misunderstanding. *Student X told the trainer that. . .* leaves no room for error.

Many people worry about whether to say 'shall' or 'will'. The grammatical rule is that, for 'I' and 'we', use 'shall' to express an ordinary future tense, and 'will' to express a stronger determination or permission. For 'you', 'he', 'she', 'it', 'they', etc, reverse this – 'will' expresses the plain future and 'shall' determination or permission.

> *I shall go tomorrow.*   *I **will** go tomorrow.*
> *The trainer will go tomorrow.*   *The trainer **shall** go tomorrow.*

The Americans, however, always use 'will' to express the plain future and 'shall' for determination or permission. It does not normally cause any confusion. If in doubt, recast the sentence. 'I am determined to go tomorrow.'

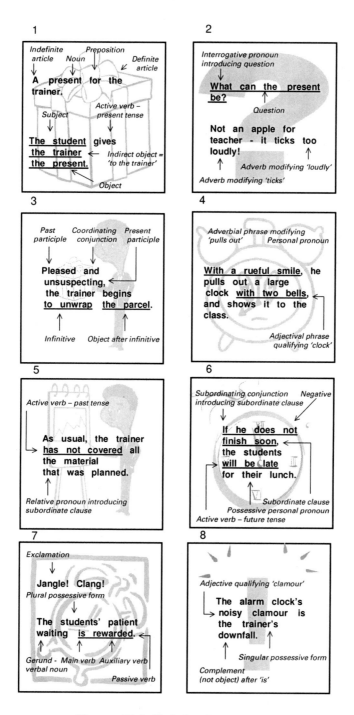

Figure 17.1 Verbal strip cartoon

Most active verbs are followed by an object on which the verb acts, an object which has, by definition, to be different from the subject of the verb. *The trainer opens the parcel.*

However, with the verb 'to be' and a few others (eg 'to seem'), the subject and the following complement (not object) refer to the same thing. *The trainer is a pleasant person.*

This can cause problems when the complement is a pronoun. We are tempted to use the accusative (object) case, eg 'It's me', rather than the nominative one (subject and complement), eg 'It's I'. 'It's me' will not normally cause any misunderstanding, but some people object to it.

Having the verb agree with its subject in number (singular or plural) can cause some difficulties. What sounds natural is usually right. Some examples will illustrate:

The students were laughing. Plural subject, so plural verb.
The number of laughing students was large. Singular subject, so singular verb.
A number of the students were laughing. 'A number of' is used as a synonym for 'many', so plural verb.
The class was in agreement. Singular subject, even though it is a collective noun, so singular verb.
The class were disagreeing amongst themselves. The context makes it clear that the singular noun is being used to mean 'the members of the class as individuals', and so the verb is plural to match.
The student and the trainer were smiling. When two parts of the subject are joined by 'and', the verb is plural.

When two parts of the subject are joined by 'or' or 'nor', the verb is singular if both are singular. If one or both are plural, make the verb agree with whichever is closer in the sentence.

Either the trainer or the student has left this.
Neither the trainer nor the students have left this.
Neither the students nor the trainer has left this.

'Each' or 'every' is always singular; 'none' may be singular or plural.

Each of the students was filled with anticipation.
There is none so deaf as he who will not hear.
None of the students were going.

Participles should be clearly attached to the nouns (or pronouns) that they qualify. Contrast these two:

Having finished their examination papers, the students left.
Having finished their examination papers, the trainer let the students go.

The second example means that the trainer completed the papers; maybe he or she marked them on the spot. There is scope for misunderstanding here. The same problem arises with the present participle. '*After finishing their examination papers. . .*'

Pronouns

There are various kinds of pronouns – personal, demonstrative ('this', 'that', 'these', 'those'), interrogative ('who', 'which', 'what', 'when', 'how' etc), and relative ('that', 'what', 'which', 'who', 'when', 'where' etc).

When using 'who' as a relative pronoun, be careful whether you are relating back to a noun which is a subject or an object (direct or indirect) – an object needs 'whom'. This may sound pedantic, and the incorrect form is unlikely to cause confusion; however it is an error many people notice.

The trainer who received the present. . .
The trainer, to whom the student gave the present. . .

Do make clear what a pronoun refers to, or you can easily create ambiguous and even absurd meanings, for example the famous: *If the baby will not drink raw milk, boil it.*

Prepositions

Prepositions are linked to nouns or pronouns, eg *to the class, after her.* Usually they precede their objects (the nouns or pronouns), but it is quite acceptable to end a sentence with a preposition, especially if the alternative sounds ridiculously tortuous.

Up to what mischief is the student getting?
Up with what tribulations must the trainer put?

Purists insist that you should not say: *Due to the student's illness, he missed seeing the trainer open the box*, but: *Owing to the student's illness. . .* There is no possibility of misunderstanding, but this is one of those usages that upset some people. You can, of course, always avoid the problem by writing: *Because the student was ill. . .*

English and US usage often differ over the use of prepositions.

English: *I spoke to Mr Jones yesterday.*
US English: *I spoke with Mr Jones yesterday.*

Adjectives and adverbs

Adjectives describe (qualify) nouns or pronouns. They come in three degrees – positive, comparative ('more. . .'), and superlative ('most. . .', '-est').

Always make comparisons perfectly clear, as they offer scope for misunderstanding.

The trainer appreciated the clock more than the student could mean either: *The trainer appreciated the clock more than the student did* or: *The trainer appreciated the clock more than he appreciated the student.*

Two comparative adjectives which are often confused are 'less' and 'fewer'. Use 'less' to make a comparative adjective negative (less surprised) and for quantity, and 'fewer' for number.

There was less time than the trainer thought.
There were fewer students than was usual.

Adverbs describe (modify) verbs or adjectives. It is important that adverbs are in the right place in the sentence otherwise the meaning can change. Contrast these three:

The happily unsuspecting trainer opened the box.
Unsuspecting, the trainer happily opened the box.
Happily, the unsuspecting trainer opened the box.

In this last example 'happily' is ambiguous – either it describes the trainer's state of mind or it can mean 'fortunately'.

Some adverbs which you need to pay special attention to placing are 'almost', 'only', 'hardly', 'wholly', 'merely'.

Phrases and clauses

Phrases are groups of words acting as single grammatical units. The position of phrases in a sentence may sometimes lead to confusion.

The students got permission to take the reports from the trainer.

Did the trainer give the students the permission or the reports or both?

Try your hand at some of these. Select the best usage.

1   Which of the two students is (taller / tallest)?
2   Repeating these tests (help / helps) to prove our point.
3   Each of the women must bear (their / her) own responsibility.
4   The Training Committee (has / have) a problem before (them / it).
5   He (has / has considered) and will consider further the student's request.
6   (There / They're / Their) absence was noticed.
7   He asked John, Bob and (I / me) to come.
8   There (was / were) a letter and a memo on the desk.
9   It looks (bad / badly).
10   The person (who / whom / with who / with whom) he met was busy.

---

1   **taller**. 'Taller' is comparative and 'tallest' is superlative. Use the superlative when referring to three or more.
2   **helps**. 'Helps' agrees with the singular subject 'repeating'.
3   **her**. 'Her' agrees with the singular pronoun 'each' .
4   **has** and **it**. Collective nouns, eg 'committee', take the singular when regarded as a unit.
5   **has considered**. You need to insert 'considered', as the two auxiliary verbs 'has' and 'will' take different forms of the main verb. Otherwise the grammatical (non)sense of the sentence is: 'He has consider and will consider further the student's request.'
6   **Their**. This is the possessive pronoun. 'There' is the opposite of 'here', and 'they're' the contraction of 'they are'.
7   **me**. This is the object of the verb 'asked'. Don't assume that 'I' is always used in a series of names.
8   **were**. 'Were' agrees with the plural complement 'letter and memo'.
9   **bad**. This is an exception to the rule that verbs are modified by adverbs. Verbs which describe senses, eg 'look', 'feel', 'taste', are modified by adjectives.
10   **whom**. The relative pronoun relates to the object of the verb 'met', and so the accusative case 'whom' should be used. 'Meet with' is colloquial, and common in the United States, but unnecessary.

Figure 17.2 Grammar exercise

Clauses must have a main verb and, usually, a subject. Phrases and clauses may perform similar grammatical functions. It is important, however, not to balance non-parallel forms – this creates a clumsy construction which can distract the reader.

Not: *To be polite or because he was curious, the trainer opened the box.*
But: *To be polite or satisfy his curiosity, the trainer opened the box.*

Conjunctions

Clauses, apart from the main clause, are introduced by conjunctions. Subordinating conjunctions (eg 'since', 'when', 'as') introduce subordinate or dependent clauses.

Coordinating conjunctions (eg 'and', 'but') introduce coordinate clauses capable of standing independently. Coordinating conjunctions are not necessary after semi-colons and colons, but they are permissible and give the second construction more emphasis. Contrast:

The trainer was curious; he therefore opened the box.
The trainer was curious; and he therefore opened the box.

Does punctuation matter?

Punctuation is often considered the poor relation of the grammar–punctuation–spelling triad, the least important of the three. But punctuation needs as much attention as grammar and spelling – maybe more, as punctuation errors are all too easy to miss in proofreading, and poor punctuation may cause misunderstanding.

The main purpose of punctuation is to make the grammatical construction, and consequently the meaning, of a piece of writing easier for the reader to understand. There have to be rules and conventions, therefore, and the principal ones are outlined in this chapter; however, there is also considerable scope for personal style.

Punctuation does visually what pause and intonation do for speech. Would you deliver a presentation in a non-stop monotone?

Full stop (.)

Do – Use a full stop to end a complete sentence.
Don't – Break sentences up into ungrammatical fragments with unnecessary and incorrect full stops.

Not: *The trainer delivered. His presentation. Very long. Very verbose. Very boring.* This could, with a certain loss of impact, be one sentence: *The trainer delivered his very long, very verbose and very boring presentation.* It could also be written as two proper sentences, this time with no loss of impact: *The trainer delivered his presentation. It was very long, very verbose and very boring.*

Don't – Follow all abbreviations with full stops, at least in the UK. In the past it was customary to use full stops after abbreviations but not after contractions (abbreviations which end in the last letter of the word). 'Mr', 'Dr', but 'Capt.', 'e.g.', 'etc.' But more and more, full stops are tending to be omitted after all abbreviations in English usage. However, full stops following all abbreviations are commonly found in US usage.

Exclamation mark (!)

Do – Use an exclamation mark instead of a full stop to end a genuine exclamation.
Do – Use it mainly in less formal documents, such as self-learning texts.
Don't – Use them just to add emphasis.
Don' t – Pepper the text with them. It becomes tedious.

Question mark (?)

Do – Use a question mark instead of a full stop to end a question.
Don't – Use it to follow an indirect question.

Not: *He asked whether the trainer gave a good presentation?*
But: *He asked whether the trainer gave a good presentation.*

Colon (:)

Do – Use a colon to introduce a list of items.
Do – Use it, as an alternative to the comma, to introduce speech. *He asked: 'Did the trainer give a good presentation?'*

Do – Use it to join two sentences or coordinate clauses. The colon gives a slightly stronger pause than the semi-colon, and may imply a contrast. It is not as common a usage as the semi-colon.

Semi-colon (;)

Do – Consider a semi-colon as a halfway house between a full stop and a comma. It can be used to link complete sentences, where you do not want the break of a full stop and where a comma would be incorrect. In particular, use it to replace a full stop if the second sentence would begin with 'and' or 'but'. *The trainer delivered his presentation; it was very long, very verbose and very boring.*
Do – Use it to separate items in a list.
Do – *Use* it. The semi-colon is one of the most versatile and underused of all the stops.

Comma (,)

Do – Use a comma to delimit a subordinate clause, a phrase or an adverb at the beginning or end of a sentence. This is not obligatory, but it helps the reader follow the sentence structure, and so grasp the meaning more easily.
Do – Similarly, use it to bracket off a subordinate clause, a phrase or an adverb in the middle of a sentence. Again this is not obligatory. Bracketing off adverbs emphasizes them.

Contrast: *Half the trainer's audience, understandably, fell asleep*
with: *Half the trainer's audience understandably fell asleep.*

This second example places less emphasis on 'understandably' and correspondingly more on 'fell asleep'.

Do – Use it to separate adjectives qualifying the same noun.
Do – Use a comma as a weaker pause than a semi-colon, when you want to join two coordinate clauses and the second begins with 'and' or 'but'.
Do – Use it as an alternative to the colon to introduce speech.
Do – Use it as an alternative to the semi-colon to separate list items.
Don't – Separate the subject from the verb, however long the sentence seems. Not: *Techniques for attracting and keeping an audience's attention and persuading, motivating and enthralling an audience, formed the substance of the trainer's presentation.* Omit the comma before 'formed'.

Don't – Use a comma to join two sentences or coordinate clauses unless the second begins with 'and' or but'. This very common error is called a 'comma fault'.

Not: *The trainer delivered his presentation as requested, it was very long, very verbose and very boring.* Replace the comma after 'requested' with a full stop or semi-colon (or possibly a colon).
Don't – Omit commas delimiting or bracketing off subordinate clauses, phrases or adverbs, where this omission may cause misunderstanding.
Not: *The trainer having finished his audience departed.* At first reading, you may wonder just how lethal the trainer's words were! The clarifying comma solves the mystery. *The trainer having finished, his audience departed.*

Brackets or parentheses ( )

Do – Use them, in preference to comma pairs, to bracket off subordinate clauses, phrases or adverbs which are truly parenthetical. They can also bracket off parenthetical sentences or whole passages.

Dash (–)

Do – Use a single dash in the same way as a colon to introduce lists. Colon dash (:-) is incorrect.
Do – Use a single or two dashes as an alternative to commas or brackets. *It was understandable – since the trainer was so boring – that half his audience fell asleep.*

Hyphen (-)

Do – Use a hyphen to join linked words where omission could cause misunder-standing. *The trainer was a long standing member of the company* suggests that corn plasters may be needed. *The trainer was a long-standing member of the company* gives a different message.
Don't – If possible, use a hyphen to break long words at the end of a line, except at the end of a syllable or between two identical consonants eg *thou-sand, mil-lion'.*
Don't – Overuse it. *End of term results* is as easily understood as *end-of-term results.*

Try your hand at punctuating the following passage. You can see my version at the beginning of the chapter, but don't imagine it is the only correct one. There is plenty of room for personal style.

does punctuation matter punctuation is often considered the poor relation of the grammar punctuation spelling triad the least important of the three but punctuation needs as much attention as grammar and spelling maybe more as punctuation errors are all too easy to miss in proofreading and poor punctuation may cause misunderstanding the main purpose of punctuation is to make the grammatical construction and consequently the meaning of a piece of writing easier for the reader to understand there have to be rules and conventions therefore and the principal ones are outlined in this chapter however there is also considerable scope for personal style punctuation does visually what pause and intonation do for speech would you deliver a presentation in a non stop monotone

Figure 17.3 Punctuation exercise

Quotation Marks (' or ")

Do – Be consistent in using single or double quotation marks. You may, however, need to use both if quoting within speech.

The trainer said: '*The manager asked me,* "*What else could I have done?*"'

Apostrophe (')

Do – Use an apostrophe to indicate possession. It goes before the additional 's' for singular nouns (and plural ones not ending in 's') , and after the plural 's' for plural nouns. It may go in either place with names ending in 's'.
The trainer's task was finished; so was Mr Jones's. The students' tasks were just beginning.
Do – Use an apostrophe to indicate the omission of letters in contracted words eg 'let's', 'don't', 'it's', 'I've'.
Don't – Use it in the possessive form of personal pronouns eg *it's* means *it is*, not *its; they're* means *they are*, not *their; who's* means *who is*, not *whose*.
Don't – Use it to indicate plurals.

Not: *DO's and DON'T's* or *do's and don't's*
But: *DOs and DON'Ts* or *dos and don'ts*

Capitals

Do – Use capital first letters for names, place names, titles and, normally, for department and company names.
Follow your house rules about using capital first letters for other words, such as product names.
Don't – Use capital first letters indiscriminately to indicate importance.

Not: The Company welcomes its Graduates to a new Training Scheme.

Note that some house rules insist that 'Company' and often 'Department' are given capital first letters, even though unqualified. Similarly, in contractual writing, defined terms are normally given capital first letters.

Spelling rules

Grammar and punctuation may allow for personal style: spelling does not. There is usually only one right way to spell a word, although some words are spelt differently in US usage, and some (not all) of these US spellings are acceptable alternatives in the UK.
   It is hardly surprising that many people find spelling a problem. There are a handful of spelling rules (we can probably all remember 'i before e except after c') but many exceptions. To complicate matters further, some words are spelt differently according to how they are used. This leads to the inescapable conclusion that the most important spelling rule of all is: look it up in a dictionary. Spelling check programs on word processors will identify for you any non-existent words you have created (and usually several existing ones too, as their dictionaries are limited), but they will not identify ones which exist but are incorrectly spelt for your meaning (eg 'practise' for 'practice'). But since it would be unbearably tedious to look every word up in a dictionary, it is worth grasping the rules and conventions that do exist.

'ie' or 'ei'

First of all 'i before e except after c' only applies to words with an 'ee' sound. Don't rely on it for words with an open 'eh' sound, eg 'leisure' (although, of course, there is always 'friend').

Exceptions are: *counterfeit, seize, weir, weird* (and *either* and *neither*, although these can be pronounced with an 'eye' sound)

'l' or 'll'

- Adjectives ending in -l or -ll form adverbs ending in -lly eg final / finally.
- Adjectives formed by adding -ful (not -full) to nouns ending in -ll, lose the second l (in English, but not necessarily in US English spelling) eg skill / skilful.
- Verbs ending in single-vowel-plus-l usually double the l in the participles and past tense (in English, but again not necessarily US English spelling) eg cancel / cancelled / cancelling. However, note that 'parallelled' and 'paralleled' are both found.

Other single or double consonants in verbs

b or bb, d or dd, m or mm, n or nn, p or pp, r or rr, s or ss, t or tt.
When these consonants are found following a *single* vowel in verbs where *the stress is on the last syllable* (eg 'ban', 'occur'), they usually double in the participles and past tense of the verb eg ban / banned / banning, occur / occurred / occurring, stop / stopped / stopping.

-ant or -ent, -ance or -ence

There are a few patterns here, but they are not really rules:

- -ate to -ant. Verbs ending in -ate usually form adjectives and nouns in -ant eg dominate / dominant.
- -ment. Nouns with this ending are common (eg improvement). -mant as a noun ending is very rare, but note 'informant'.
- -scent. This ending for adjectives is always -scent, never -scant, as in 'acquiescent'.
- -ance or -ence. Many -ance or -ence nouns are linked with -ant or -ent adjectives, and so follow the same patterns, few as they are eg dominant / dominance, acquiescent / acquiescence. However, there are other -ance and -ence nouns too, where there is no easily distinguishable pattern or guide eg maintenance, preference.

The best source of help really is your dictionary.

-tion or -sion

-tion is the more common ending. -sion is found in nouns derived from *some* verbs ending in:

- -end eg comprehend / comprehension. But note 'intend' which gives 'intention'.
- -ise eg supervise / supervision.
- -de eg divide / division.
- -rt eg convert / conversion. But note that 'insert' gives 'insertion'.
- -ede or -eed eg succeed / succession.
- -it eg permit / permission.

-able or -ible

The question is not only which of these two suffixes you choose, but also whether they alter the spelling of the noun or verb to which they are attached.

In general, -able seems the more common suffix. -ible is often used to create adjectives from the same groups of verbs which gave nouns ending in -sion. (However, these also frequently form adjectives in -ive.) Note for example: comprehend / comprehensible; convert / convertible; divide / divisible; permit / permissible; supervise / supervisible. Once more, I recommend the dictionary.

This, obviously, would dispose of the second problem too, but for those of you seeking general guidelines on how -able, in particular, affects the spelling of its preceding verbs:

- Verbs ending in -ate often drop this eg irritate / irritable.
- Verbs ending in consonant-plus-e often drop the e eg advise / advisable.
- However, verbs ending in -ce and -ge keep the e eg manage / manageable.
- Verbs ending in consonant-plus-y change the y to i eg rely / reliable. But, the inevitable exception, 'apply' gives 'applicable'.

Plurals

Most English nouns form their plurals in -s or -es.

- For nouns ending in consonant-plus-y (but not vowel-plus-y), the y becomes i before adding -es eg sky / skies, tray / trays.
- Some nouns ending in -o add an e before the plural -s; others don't eg potato / potatoes, avocado / avocados.

- Some nouns ending in –f have their plural forms ending in -fs; others claim -ves; still others can take either ending eg proof / proofs, knife / knives.
- Nouns ending in –ch, -s, -sh, -ss, or -x normally take -es for their plurals eg box / boxes, guess / guesses, summons / summonses.
- However, some nouns ending in –s, such as series, remain unchanged in the plural.
- Nouns ending in –ix normally make their plurals in –ices eg appendix / appendices. But 'prefix' gives 'prefixes'.

And, to add to the variation, there are also, of course, many totally irregular plurals – the answer remains the same: consult your dictionary.

Negatives

Negative prefixes are added to verbs, nouns, adjectives and adverbs. There is no standard negative prefix.

- Verbs can form their negatives with:
  - de- eg decipher;
  - dis- eg disagree;
  - un- eg undo.
- Negative verbs beginning with mis- (eg misjudge) imply 'bad' rather then 'not'.
- Nouns can form their negatives with:
  - de- eg decomposition;
  - dis- eg disbelief;
  - non- eg non-delivery ('non-' is usually hyphenated, but there are exceptions, such as nonsense).
- Again, negatives beginning with mis- (eg misdemeanour) imply 'bad'.
- Adjectives, and hence adverbs derived from them, can form their negatives with:
  - dis- eg dishonest;
  - ig- eg ignoble;
  - in- eg indecent;
  - un- eg unhappy.
- Adjectives beginning with m- or p- usually form their negatives with im- eg immature, impolite.
- Adjectives beginning with l- use il- eg illegible.
- Adjectives beginning with r- similarly use ir- eg irrelevant.

- Some adjectives have negative forms beginning with non- (hyphenated) eg non-stick.
- As with verbs and nouns, mis- means 'bad' eg misused, which can be compared to unused or disused.

Abbreviations

Some standard abbreviations are often confused and misspelt.

- cf means 'compare with';
- etc means 'and others';
- eg means 'for example';
- ie means 'that is';
- NB means '*nota bene*' or note well.

US spellings

No chapter discussing English spelling would be complete without a comment on US variations. In general, where US spellings differ, they are simpler and more straightforward than English ones.

For instance, in English spelling, words like practice / practise often cause problems. In US spelling, however, the -ce ending serves for both verb and noun.

The main differences between English and US spelling are:

- English -our/US -or eg colour / color.
- English -ise or -ize/US -ize eg rationalise / rationalize.
- English -re/US -er eg metre / meter.
- English ae and oe diphthongs/US e eg manoeuvre / maneuver.
- English ll in verb forms and some nouns and adjectives/US l eg levelled / leveled. (But English skilful becomes US skillful!)

I have been stressing the importance of using a dictionary, but some misspellings may become so entrenched in your mind that you are not aware that they are incorrect, and therefore see no need to look them up. Try your hand at the exercise in Figure 17.4 with 20 commonly misspelt words, and remember always to look up any you get wrong!

Which of these forms is correct?

accommodate	acommodate	accomodate
apalled	apauled	appalled
calander	calendar	calender
commemorate	comemorate	commemmorate
committee	commitee	comittee
concensus	consensus	consensous
correspondence	corespondance	correspondance
decisive	dicisive	desisive
delapidated	dilapidated	dillapidated
embarass	embarrass	embarace
fortuitious	fortiutious	fortuitous
homoginious	homogeneous	homogenious
laboratory	laboratary	laborotary
ocurrence	ocurrance	occurrence
parallel	paralell	parallell
recommend	reccommend	recomend
rhinoseros	rhinoscerous	rhinoceros
suptle	sutle	subtle
surreptitious	sureptitious	sureptitous
temporery	temperary	temporary

Answers

accommodate	appalled	calendar	commemorate
committee	consensus	correspondence	decisive
dilapidated	embarrass	fortuitous	homogeneous
laboratory	occurrence	parallel	recommend
rhinoceros	subtle	surreptitious	temporary

Figure 17.4 Spelling exercise

Conclusion

By now, I fear, you may be feeling totally confused and wondering how you ever manage to express anything correctly. But much of this comes naturally to people for whom English is the first language, and the more widely you read the better your grammar, punctuation and spelling are likely to be. Bad grammar, punctuation, and spelling do matter – they give an unprofessional or careless image to what you write – and they are avoidable. Dictionaries and thesauruses, computer grammar and spelling checks (despite their limitations) are all quick and easy to use.

18

Tables and Charts

Summary

This chapter looks at different ways of presenting numerical information, including the use of computer chart packages, different chart formats, and the situations most suitable for each. It considers the following formats:

- tables;
- line graphs;
- bar and column charts;
- pie charts;
- organization charts;
- flowcharts;
- decision trees.

Tables

There are many ways of presenting numbers, and the way you choose can significantly influence your reader's understanding and interpretation.

The most commonly chosen, although sometimes the least helpful way, is the table.

Tables have many good points, and others not so good. Among the advantages are:

- They are easy to prepare.
- They can include a lot of information.
- They can be used to compare many variables over two or three dimensions.

Table 18.1 Example table

COURSE PARTICIPANTS 1995–2001

	1995	1996	1997	1998	1999	2000	2001	Total
Supervisory Skills – participants	25	20	24	24	10	30	35	168
– dropouts	4	3	4	4	4	2	3	24
Induction – participants	34	38	38	42	30	45	65	292
– dropouts	8	5	6	6	12	10	13	60
Effective Writing – participants	-	-	-	-	-	15	25	40
– dropouts	-	-	-	-	-	2	2	4
Total – participants	59	58	62	66	40	90	125	500
– dropouts	12	8	10	10	16	14	18	88

In Table 18.1, the dimensions shown are years and numbers (of participants/ dropouts), and the different courses are the variables.

The big disadvantages of tables are that you can easily include *too much* information in them and it can be difficult to identify exactly what is important.

Of course, this can be an advantage if you are trying to camouflage any poor results, such as the high drop-out level in 1999. Table 18.1 is a horrible table, a jumble of figures thrown together without considering how the reader will use them. Changes in the order, spacing to emphasize the structure of the table or significant aspects, a key or notes explaining particular points, the use of percentages or averages rather than raw numbers – these all aid interpretation. Nor need figures always be precise; often the general impression gained from rounded figures is more important than three places of decimals. Table 18.2 is more communicative.

Line graphs

Table 18.2 is still not ideal, however. You are using it to try to compare the size of several variables but this can be better done pictorially. Line graphs used to be unpopular with writers because of the difficulty of preparation, a painstaking, manual task which could not always be delegated to a secretary. The advent of spreadsheet computer packages has made a great difference. These can be linked to word processing packages and used to present raw numbers in various forms, including line graphs.

If you are able to use colour on graphs, you can increase the clarity and even the number of variables. However, colour reproduction is beyond the scope of many trainers for normal use. Nevertheless, by using different line forms, different point marks, or different hatching patterns, you can distinguish up to eight variables quite adequately in black and white (which is more than enough for one graph!). Indeed, there is undoubtedly too much information on this graph, and it would be better to use several short versions covering only the particular variables you want to compare at any point, for instance Induction participants and Total participants.

Lines on a graph can be zigzag (with straight lines connecting each point) or smoothed out into curves. You can also show a trend line or a 'line of best fit'.

Note that the line graph can give you a visual appreciation of average values over all variables. In Figure 18.1 the averages are obviously somewhere between the levels of the Induction and Supervisory Skills participants.

Table 18.2 Improved table

Course Participants 1995–2001

	1995	1996	1997	1998	1999	2000	2001	Ave
Induction — participants	34	38	38	42	30	45	65	42
— dropouts %*	19%	12%	14%	13%	**29%**	18%	17%	17%
Supervisory Skills — participants	25	20	24	24	10	30	35	24
— dropout %*	14%	13%	14%	14%	**29%**	6%	8%	12%
Effective Writing — participants	-	-	-	-	-	15	25	40
— dropout %*	-	-	-	-	-	12%	7%	9%
Total — participants	59	58	62	66	40	90	125	500
— dropout %*	17%	12%	14%	13%	**29%**	13%	13%	15%

* % of total nominations

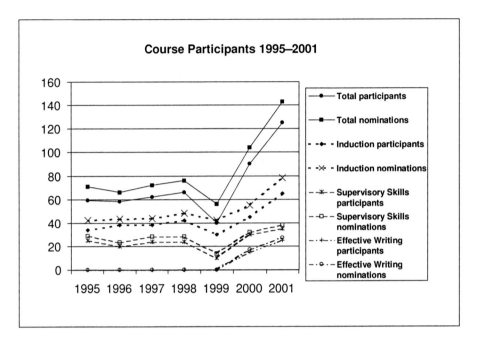

Figure 18.1 Line graph

Bar and column charts

Bar charts run horizontally across the page, while column charts are vertical. Typically that means that you can have more bars than columns on a chart, but otherwise there is little to choose between these two formats. They convey less information than tables or graphs, but do give considerable impact.

Pie charts

Whereas line graphs and bar and column charts compare size, pie charts show proportion. They are divided into slices which make up the whole, preferably not more than five or six, otherwise labelling each slice becomes awkward without a key. To emphasize one particular slice, cut it out of the pie.

Organization charts

These show 'family trees', both of genealogical development and of job reporting structures. Unlike real trees, they 'grow' vertically down from the top, the biggest problem being how to fit in all the 'branches' at one level. Options are:

Figure 18.2 Bar chart

Figure 18.3 Column chart

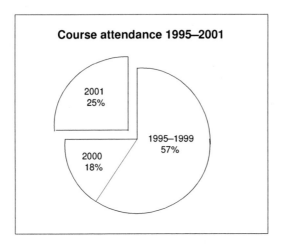

Figure 18.4 Pie chart

- Reducing type size as you work down the chart. This has obvious limitations.
- Spreading branches at the same level over two or more lines.
- Switching from horizontal to vertical presentation for the bottom level.
- Removing the development of one or more branches from the main chart and presenting them as separate organization charts.

These last three options are all shown in Figure 18.5. Do be wary, though, of organization charts as cluttered as this one. Keep information to the necessary minimum by omitting the detail of any branches which are less important for your purpose. Exclude also any details which are likely to change frequently, for instance job holders' names – updating organization charts can be time-consuming, and out-of-date charts are positively dangerous.

Obviously, you would not, in one chart, normally use three different ways of dealing with the 'too many branches at one level' problem. The best choice, in this case, would be the middle one, with a general organization chart showing the relationship between the departments, and three separate ones for the Information Services, Finance, and Human Resources functions.

Unbroken lines on organization charts show a direct reporting relationship; broken or dotted lines normally show a secondary or staff relationship. These can easily over-complicate a chart, however, so unless they are really necessary, avoid them and simply mention the secondary relationship as a footnote.

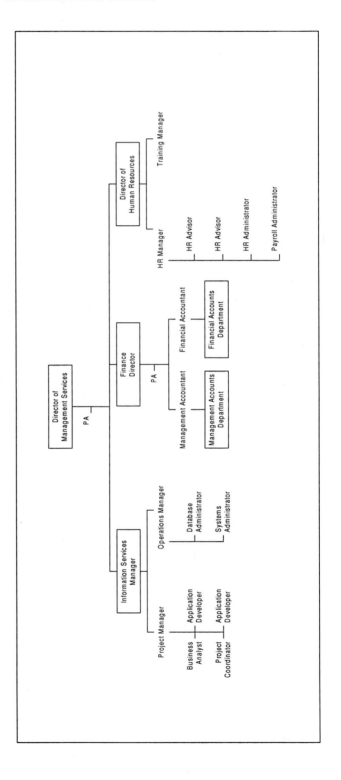

Figure 18.5 Organization chart

Flowcharts

These show the progression of an activity. Common in Information Services applications, they are also extremely useful for other areas. In particular, they can be an excellent alternative to lengthy procedures and job aids.

There are many standard flowchart symbols and, although some of these may not be relevant to training applications, the more common ones are worth learning and using correctly.

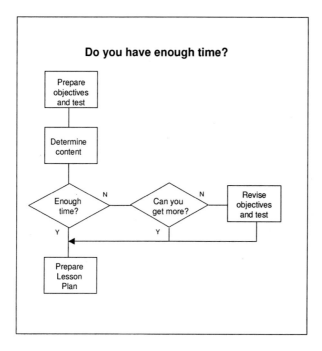

Figure 18.6 Flowchart

Decision trees

These look like organization charts although, equally unnaturally, they often grow from left to right. In function, they combine the organization chart's representation of dependent relationships and the flowchart's progress picture. They identify the different options available at any point, their likely outcomes, and any consequent options for each of the outcomes etc. Maze exercises can all be plotted as decision trees. However, their greatest use is as decision-making tools, where they can be combined with numerical weightings.

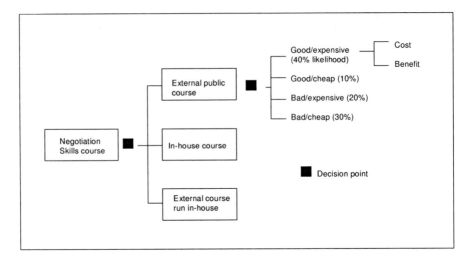

Figure 18.7 Decision tree

The decision tree in the next example examines the options for a writing skills course. Each of the options is divided into different possible outcomes with their presumed likelihood and costs/benefits. These could be used to calculate an overall 'best' choice .

Clearly, a decision tree can easily get very complicated. As with organization charts, it is often helpful to present a simplified global chart, with each of the branches developed as sub-charts.

Chart packages

Spreadsheet packages offer you the option of turning your spreadsheets into chart formats. Presentation packages also offer many charting options. And you can frequently incorporate these charts straight into your word processing package. These are all fairly straightforward to use and manipulate, in order to get the precise effect that you want. They are probably sufficient for most trainers' needs, but, if required, there are also specialist packages for process and flowcharts and for organization charts.

19

Using Technology

Summary

Technology has frequently been mentioned in previous chapters, but this chapter summarizes the various technological aids the trainer/writer may want to use, and the opportunities they offer:

- Word processors. These are now ubiquitous and they are an enormous improvement on typewriters. Editing is easy; spelling mistakes diminish, even if they do not disappear completely; and the finished product looks good.
- Spreadsheet packages. These allow you to manipulate and present numerical information in different ways, including pictorial charts.
- Presentation packages. At the very least, the trainer should aim to master a presentation package – in the long run, it is much easier than having someone else interpret your ideas. These packages include graphics elements, and allow you to add animation and other media elements too.
- Desktop publishing (DTP). Use DTP to pull text and graphics together to produce professional looking documents. It is particularly useful for self-learning texts.
- The Internet and company networks. These give the trainer many facilities, including information sources, ways to market the training function, automated training records and e-learning courses.

Word processing

A word processing package stores typed text on a computer, so that it can be copied, searched and edited freely. Word processing packages have revolutionized the production of written materials.

The most important point, for you as a writer, is that you can edit properly without being constrained by the thought:'Dare I insert this paragraph on page one, and so force my secretary to retype the next six pages too?' With a word processor, you have total freedom to change what you have written, to move a passage from one part of the document to another, or to alter your layout completely.

Of course, that is no reason for giving your secretary scrappy or ill-prepared first drafts. However, it is often easier to judge how a document reads once it is typed, and in reality word processing drafts are, and should be, submitted at an earlier stage than those for typewriter production.

In fact, many trainers now produce their own materials, rather than having them produced by a secretary or assistant. Two- or four-finger typing is quite adequate, and the word processing packages themselves are very 'user-friendly'.

But what about those of us who freeze at the sight of a computer screen and keyboard? It is worth overcoming this reluctance with private practice. It is virtually impossible to wreck any modern computer system; and most user manuals are now very simply and clearly expressed and include basic tuition packages designed to give the user the skill and confidence to experiment further. Remember, it is not necessary to be a trained typist.

Word processors also offer a variety of useful language aids. The one most commonly used is a spelling check. This does not guarantee that all the words in the document are correctly spelt. What the spelling check does is compare each word with the word processor's inbuilt dictionary. If a word is 'not found', you can correct your spelling or add your word to the dictionary. However, the spelling check will not pick up 'we' (when you meant 'wet') or 'peace' (for 'piece'). Do make sure your checker is not automatically set to US English if you are in the UK. Incidentally, most spelling checks give you a word count, which can be useful.

Other language aids are:

- A Thesaurus, giving you words of similar meaning.
- A grammar check. Similar to the spelling check, this checks your sentence structure and punctuation against preset rules and formats. Sometimes these may seem rather archaic, depending on the type of document you are writing. You can, if you wish, ignore the suggested corrections.
- A style check. These are not always included in word processing packages but are available separately. They tend to perform the equivalent of a FOG Index, concentrating on sentence and word length, and also the use of passive verbs. Some style checks offer suggested alternative versions.
- A further facility, which can be helpful with long documents, is contents listing and indexing. This is achieved by searching the document for key words.

Spreadsheet packages

These are designed to allow you to store, retrieve, calculate and display large quantities of numerical information. The standard display format is a tabular one, but most spreadsheet packages will also present the information as a line graph, a bar or column chart, or a pie chart. The sizes of the bars, columns or pie slices, and the exact slope of the graph lines will be calculated for you by the package.

Many word processing and spreadsheet packages can be linked, so that spreadsheet information can be incorporated into a word processed document.

Presentation packages

Even if you do not feel it worthwhile to become expert with a word processor, learning to use a presentation package will transform your visuals. Presentation packages help you to produce attractive and professional looking charts, graphs, drawings and course visuals.

Let's look at a few examples. In Chapter 18, I suggested that pie charts are an excellent way of showing proportions. Compare the simple pie chart, produced manually, with the one produced by the presentation package.

Similarly, in Chapter 9, I suggested that stick men are perfectly adequate in cartoon drawings. So they are, but a presentation package will offer you a range of super-stick men.

Presentation packages offer a variety of lettering styles and sizes for headings and text, and a gallery of ready-drawn shapes and pictures for you to choose from. You can also draw your own pictures straight onto the computer screen and scan in pictures or photographs using an electronic scanner.

 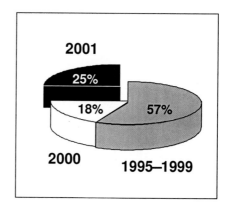

Figure 19.1 Hand-drawn and presentation package pie charts

Figure 19.2 Hand-drawn and presentation package cartoons

Amongst the visual effects which can be produced by most packages are:

- 3D charts;
- drop shadows (a shadow below and beside the drawing, letter or symbol) to give emphasis;
- variable shading, of a gradual, regularly increasing or decreasing intensity;
- a wide range of colours;
- backgrounds and borders;
- animation, both of slide transitions and of picture elements;
- inclusion of other media elements, such as audio or video material.

Presentation packages are built around slides, which can be produced in a variety of formats (paper, overhead transparencies, 35mm slides) depending on your output devices, and also as an on-screen show. Notes pages can be added to the slides, and the slides can be printed in handout form.

Although presentation packages are more complicated than word processing ones, it is worth learning to use one yourself. Otherwise you are dependent on somebody else's interpretation of your ideas, which, with such an enormous range of options available, may be very different from what you intended.

DTP

Word processed text looks attractive but ordinary. You can enhance the appearance by good layout and illustrations, but the effect is workmanlike and efficient rather than smoothly impressive. Where presentation is critical, you can improve on word processing by using a DTP package.

What might you use it for? The most obvious application would be self-learning texts, but it is also invaluable for forms and questionnaires, job aids, and course catalogues.

To see what a DTP package can achieve, consider the sample pages from a self-learning text which I used as an illustration in Chapter 12. They were created with word processed text and hand-drawn illustrations, physically cut-and-pasted to make up the page. The result is perfectly adequate for in-house training materials. It is not, however, as professional looking or as inviting to use as the desktop publishing version.

DTP combines text and graphics – the text may be ready word processed and the graphics prepared using a graphics package, or they may both be created using the DTP package itself.

Significant features are:

- Various styles and sizes of lettering can be used.
- Text can be laid out in several columns and, if desired, justified. (The spaces between the words are expanded or contracted so that each line of text fills the complete width of the column.)
- Text can flow round the graphics, enclosing their shape.
- Various colours can be used, depending on the capabilities of your printer.

Graphics and picture editing packages

These allow you to edit and play with pictures, whether drawn by yourself, downloaded from a picture library or scanned in, to create the effects you want. The pictures can then be incorporated into materials prepared through presentation or DTP packages.

Computer networks

Networks, be they the Internet or your company network, can be used for a number of purposes:

- Research. It sometimes seems as if there is *everything* on the Internet (and that your search engine is bringing up everything except the one document you really need!). Although searching for information on the Internet can be time-consuming, nevertheless it is an excellent source of material and ideas.

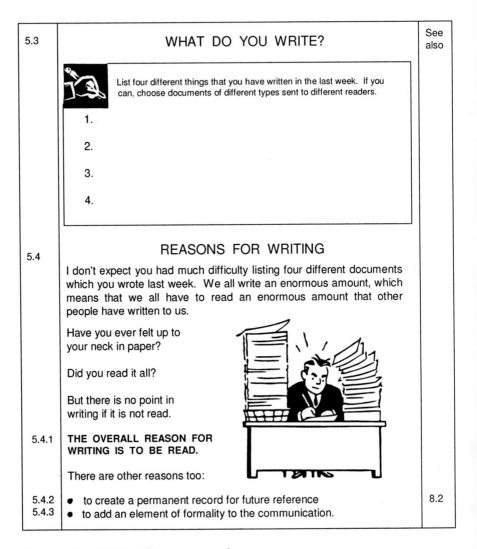

Figure 19.3 DTP self-learning product page

- Marketing your training function. Setting up your own Web page, even if only on your company network, makes it easy for your users to understand the services that you can provide. Making the site look attractive, easy to use and professional is essential for the success of your marketing.
- Maintaining training records. You can set up an automatic course booking system, so that training course participants can automatically book themselves onto courses, or subscribe to self-learning material. Attendance/completion of self-learning materials and, if desired, test results can also be logged, so that complete training records can be kept.

Writing to be Read

We all write an enormous amount, which means that we all have to read an enormous amount that other people have written to us.

Do you read everything in your in-tray? But there is no point in writing if it is not read.

THE OVERALL REASON FOR WRITING IS TO BE READ.

There are other reasons too:

- to create a permanent record for future reference
  (For more information on archiving materials, click here.)

- to make the communication more formal.

Have you ever felt up to your neck in paper?

Figure 19.4 Web self-learning product page

- Accessing e-learning programmes. Electronic self-learning materials may be bought off-the-shelf or designed to fit your needs. Special authoring or 'learning management' systems are required. This is a very technical area, and trainers may wish to seek the help of their IT departments in the first instance. Self-learning texts which you design yourself for delivery via the Web may look quite different from the paper-based equivalent, because of the constraints and added features inherent in Web design. Figure 19.4 shows part of the same self-learning page as a Web product.

APPENDIX 1

Further Reading

Writing

Buzan, T (1974) *Use Your Head*, BBC Books, London

Carey, G V (1976) *Mind the Stop*, Penguin Books, Harmondsworth

Chambers Concise Dictionary (1990), Chambers, Lonson

The Concise Oxford English Dictionary (1990), Oxford University Press, Oxford

Gowers, Sir Ernest, rev S Greenbaum and J Whitcut (1986) *The Complete Plain Words*, Penguin Books, Harmondsworth

Hart, H (1983) *Hart's Rules for Compositors and Readers*, 39th edition, Oxford University Press, Oxford

Huff, Darrell (1973) *How to Lie with Statistics*, Penguin Books, Harmondsworth

Partridge, E (1973) *Usage and Abusage*, Penguin Books, Harmondsworth

The Right Word at the Right Time (1985) The Reader's Digest Association, London

Roget's Thesaurus (1987) Penguin Books, Harmondsworth

Thomson, A J and Martinet, A V (1990) *Oxford Pocket English Grammar*, Oxford University Press, Oxford

Training materials

Barker, Alan (1999) *Writing at Work*, Industrial Society, London

Business, Commerce and Industry (1980) Dynamic Graphics, Inc

Corder, Colin (1990) *Teaching Hard, Teaching Soft*, Gower, Aldershot

Elton, Jackie (1988) *Letter Writing*, Industrial Society, London

Fletcher, Shirley (1997) *Analysing Competence*, Kogan Page, London

Jay, Antony (1976) *Slide Rules*, Video Arts

Mager, Robert (1990) *Preparing Instructional Objectives*, Kogan Page, London

National Standards for Training and Development (1991) Training and Development Lead Body, Sheffield

Race, Phil (1989) *The Open Learning Handbook*, Kogan Page, London

Ravet, Serge and Layte, Maureen (1998) *Technology-Based Training*, Kogan Page, London

Ross, Susannah (2001) *A Simple Guide to Writing for your Website*, Prentice Hall, London

Stevens, Michael (ed) (1990) *Case Studies*, BACIE, London

Ungerson, Bernard (1983) *How to Write a Job Description*, Institute of Personnel Management, London

Vidal-Hall, Judith (1988) *Report Writing*, Industrial Society, London

APPENDIX 2

Useful Web Sites

about.com – useful search engine
www.ask.co.uk – useful search engine
www.cbi.org.uk – CBI Web site
www.cipd.co.uk – CIPD Web site
www.dreamink.com – advice on designing Web materials
www.google.com – useful search engine
www.indsoc.co.uk – Industrial Society Web site
www.inst-mgt.org.uk – Institute of Management Web site
www.patent.gov.uk – information on copyright
www.plainenglish.co.uk – Plain English Campaign Web site
useit.com – advice on designing Web materials
webpagesthatsuck.com – advice on designing Web materials

APPENDIX 3

Information Services

Chartered Institute of Personnel and Development, CIPD House, Camp Road, London SW19 4UX

Confederation of British Industry, Centre Point, 103 New Oxford Street, London WC1A 1DU

Industrial Society, Peter Runge House, 3 Carlton House Terrace, London SW1Y 5DG

Institute of Management, Management House, Cottingham Road, Corby, Northants NN17 1TT

National Council for Educational Technology, 3 Devonshire Street, London W1N 2BA

Plain English Campaign, PO Box 3, New Mills, High Peak, SK22 4QB

Training and Development Lead Body, The Employment Department, Qualifications and Standards Branch (QS7), Room E704, Moorfoot, Sheffield S1 4PQ

Index

NB: page numbers in *italics* indicate figures or tables